Commentary on the Belgic Confession

By Dr. Chuck Baynard

Bible Quotes are from the AV 1769 edition

Full Bible Publications

Manassas * Clover

2

ISBN 978-0-6151-8825-6

INTRODUCTION

The Belgic Confession of Faith – This Reformed Confession was prepared in 1561 by [Guido] de Bres (c.1523-1567), who was later martyred, others, then slightly revised by Francis Junius (1545-1602) of Bourges. First written in French, it was soon translated into Dutch and Latin. The Synod of Dort (1618-1619) made a revision but did not change the doctrine. It covers the spectrum of theological topics.

Though the dates of publication are close (within 2-3 years, 1559 & 1561) a distinct maturity of doctrine can be seen between the *French and Belgic Confessions*. Whereas a comparison of the French to the Second Helvetic reveals these two retain much of the same subject matter and phraseology (1559 & 1566). Surprisingly it is the document in the middle of this scant 7 year period that is the most complete and has the terminology carried forward into the 17th century confessional documents (*Heidelberg Catechism* 1563).

The various Confessions from the founders of the Reformation contain the seed of the Reformation and are very valid for the Reformed churches today. They are a necessity in understanding who we are and passing the Reformed faith to the next generation.

A proper understanding of the doctrines of the Reformation will hold our churches solidly within Biblical guidelines. The shout today for more contemporary confessions is a false hope. Knowing who we are and contending for the faith once delivered will restore our churches. Most of the heresies of the sixteenth century have assumed new names and are a thorn in the side of the bride of Christ today even as they were 500 years ago.

Another consideration has been what I perceive to be the unity of the Reformed confessions through the centuries rather than a different perspective of God and His works, as some hold exists between these early continental reformers and their later English brothers. These differences are more cultural and ethnic than a difference of theology. A study of all of the key literature of the confessional documents will reveal a line of debarkation from the traditional Roman Catholic excesses and a return to the Bible that can be seen as one and a continuing maturity of theology and not a difference as such in approach or thought. The theology expressed here wears well on either side of the English Channel and in my opinion is centerline with all Confessions. Where I differ from the majority of others it is noted in the text.

The following abbreviations are used in the footnotes:

HC Heidelberg Catechism

H 2nd Helvetic Confession of Faith

WCF Westminster Confession of Faith

WSC Westminster Shorter Catechism

WLC Westminster Larger Catechism

D Canons of Dort

Cross-references are made to other Reformed Confessions in an attempt to show the harmony of the various standards. I owe Dr. Joel Beeke a great deal of thanks for his work in *Reformed Confessions Harmonized*. Dr. Beeke's harmony cut research time to nil and the annotated bibliography in the same book provided invaluable references to the works of others to test my theology against to help insure I held the middle line of Reformed thought.[1] In passing, this is the best harmony of Reformed confessions in existence in my opinion and an absolute necessity for Reformed pastors.

Questions have been added at the end of each article in an attempt to guide the reader to the most salient points of each article.

Along with a free flowing commentary I have also tried to give attention to the original intent of the reformers where culture or circumstance indicates there may be extenuating circumstances involved. It would take several volumes to produce an exegesis as such of every article of the Confession. That is not the intent of this treatment. The intent here is to bring to the forefront the essential doctrines of the confession that the church must understand today if she is to faithfully contend for the faith. It is also an attempt to present a primer that the contemporary urban

---

[1] Beeke, Joel & Ferguson, Sinclair, Ed. *Reformed Confessions Harmonized.* Baker Books, Grand Rapids 1999, 2000

audience can understand and accept. We find ourselves in the midst of a generation where for the most part few have an understanding of church history or theological constructions. Ignorance of any particular area will produce in man one of two reactions. What a person does not understand will be treated indifferently or completely ignored. The church can ill afford either of these luxuries. I pray I can aptly express to the churches the crucial nature of at least a basic understanding of our Confessions by all of her members. This desire also limits the over all size that this volume can occupy. I have attempted to provide enough references in the footnotes to other Confessions to at least guide the more ardent student to the materials to obtain a deeper understanding than perhaps I have been able to convey here.

I remain convinced that the solution to the church's problems today lie within her creeds and history. They must assume their rightful place alongside the Scripture as the guide of our understanding of God's will for us.

The Belgic Confession of Faith, Article I

There Is Only One God

We all believe with the heart and confess with the mouth that there is one only simple and spiritual Being, which we call God; and that He is eternal, incomprehensible, invisible, immutable, infinite, almighty, perfectly wise, just, good, and the overflowing fountain of all good.

And God spoke all these words, saying: I am the LORD your God, who brought you out of the land of Egypt, out of the house of bondage. "You shall have no other gods before Me. You shall not make for yourself a carved image, or any likeness of anything that is in heaven above, or that is in the earth beneath, or that is in the water under the earth; you shall not bow down to them nor serve them. For I, the LORD your God, am a jealous God, visiting the iniquity of the fathers on the children to the third and fourth generations of those who hate Me, but showing mercy to thousands, to those who love Me and keep My commandments. (Exodus 20:1-6)

You are My witnesses," says the LORD, "And My servant whom I have chosen, That you may know and believe Me, And understand that I am He. Before Me there was no God formed, Nor shall there be after Me. (Isa. 43:10)[2]

In the first commandment God says there shall be no other gods before me. This does not mean there is another god that we may choose. There is no clash of the Titans as one god seeks to wrest control from another. Isaiah[3] is very clear about this. In Isaiah we also notice another great truth, all that we can know about God is what God has revealed about Himself. All mankind does not equally understand the Bible. It takes the supernatural

---

[2] HC Q94; Q95- H III.1-2 - WCF II - WSC Q4; Q5 - WLC Q6; Q7; Q8

[3] Isaiah 43:10

revelation of God the Holy Spirit for man to see this truth about God. Speaking of man in general, man has recognized that he is not the superior force in the universe and has sought to create images of these perceived powers and to worship these images.[4] When another person or event revealed a perceived god to the natural man, this natural man added this new god to his collection of gods. Among the ancient peoples only Israel was monotheistic, that is, had only one God. The incident concerning the Ark of the Covenant reveals the attempt of that pagan people to simply add the living God to their system of gods whom they served.[5]

The Belgic Confession at this point continues with the names of some of the attributes of God. First, God has only revealed Himself in His attributes or personality as they have been revealed both by name and by God's interaction with mankind.[6] The conclusion then that God is the only God and from God alone comes all good is a reasonable and logical conclusion.

John Calvin in the *Institutes of the Christian Religion* begins book one with a treatment of the knowledge of God and concludes that natural man when he considers the world around him will decide there is a God from the complexity yet simplicity of order in nature. Calvin also concludes that as man turns inward and examines himself, man's eyes will be drawn upward toward God and man will come to the same conclusion from his own being that there is a created order and this order demands a God of creation. Thus the statement that man cannot know himself until he knows God because man is created in the image of God. This is in agreement with Paul in Romans one and leaves all of mankind guilty before God, conceived and born in sin, condemned already by their own hand[7].

The rallying cry of Israel, "Hear O' Israel, the LORD your

---

[4] Romans 1

[5] 1 Sam 5

[6] While man may not live by experience, experience has a place in the proper study and understanding of God. I find Romans 5:1-5 is a prime example of the place man's experience has in the theological scheme of things. (Rom. 5:1 Therefore being justified by faith, we have peace with God through our Lord Jesus Christ: 2 By whom also we have access by faith into this grace wherein we stand, and rejoice in hope of the glory of God. 3 And not only so, but we glory in tribulations also: knowing that tribulation worketh patience; 4 And patience, experience; and experience, hope: 5 And hope maketh not ashamed; because the love of God is shed abroad in our hearts by the Holy Ghost which is given unto us.

[7] Institutes 1.1

GOD is one GOD," is the battle cry of the church today in a sea of humanity seeking peace with a world at war with God. The body of Christ (The church) has only one head, even Jesus Christ and cannot embrace other so-called world religions as another alternative. Christianity is not an inclusive religion, but is explicitly exclusive of all but the worship of the only living God who created all things for His own glory alone.[8]

Questions

1. How/where does God reveal His personality to us?

2. Why can it be said that Christianity is an exclusive religion?

3. According to Calvin what may man consider that will lead him to believe there is a Creator God?

---

[8] Rom 1:20; Jer. 10:12; Psa. 33:5; 104:24

The Belgic Confession of Faith, Article II

By What Means God Is Made Known unto Us

We know Him by two means: First, by the creation, preservation, and government of the universe; which is before our eyes as a most elegant book, wherein all creatures, great and small, are as so many characters leading us to see clearly the invisible things of God, even his everlasting power and divinity, as the apostle Paul says (Rom. 1:20). All which things are sufficient to convince men and leave them without excuse. Second, He makes Himself more clearly and fully known to us by His holy and divine Word, that is to say, as far as is necessary for us to know in this life, to His glory and our salvation.[9]

We touched on this in the commentary on Article 1. The main consideration here is to distinguish general knowledge about God through nature from special revelation of God as revealed in the Bible.[10] Nature reveals enough about the existence of God that no man can claim not to know God exists. Paul goes so far in Romans[11] to say that by the light of nature alone man even knows about the invisible things of God to include God's power and of the Godhead (Trinity), without any of the revealed word of God being present.[12] Thereby all mankind stands condemned by the sure knowledge of God all can obtain from nature. Note that this natural revelation however does not include the knowledge of God's plan of redemption or introduce the Savior and thus the light of nature alone cannot save man. *Faith comes from hearing and hearing from the word of God.* The early church took this verse to heart so deeply that at one point Augustine declared since they

---

[9] HC Q122 - WCF I.1 - WLC Q2 - D Head 3-4 Art 6-7

[10] I consider Calvin's conclusions concerning man's ability to know there is a God by considering himself to be part of the natural revelation of nature, not another addition to how we know there is a God.

[11] Romans 1 all

[12] This is an important truth of the Bible that mankind seems to have difficulty grasping. This is crucial to understanding and accepting original sin. This makes the truth of the fall and man's inability to save self visible to us. This is in perfect alignment with Calvin's suggestion man will when examining self immediately look upward and know there is a God.

could not hear the deaf could not be saved.

This might seem like we are beating a dead horse so to speak, but that all mankind is condemned already needs to be understood. The hard doctrines of the Bible (no they are not an exclusive of Calvinism) will not be accepted by man without the foundation of understanding that all mankind is doomed to the fires of hell already and there is no way man can save himself. Total depravity[13] is a God revealed truth. It is only with this understanding the necessity of grace, the election and the sending of His Son as our Redeemer will make sense to the finite mind of the created.

To a mankind condemned and assigned to the judgment of hell God reached out in grace choosing some to eternal salvation in Jesus Christ His only begotten Son. Love and mercy as revealed in grace precede all acts of salvation to include the election. The others God passed over. Some point to a decree of reprobation here. This is an error; all mankind was condemned already and deserving of the fires of hell. There was no need for God to do anything to bring this about; the sin is laid at the feet of the created, not God.[14]

God having used the dual revelation of Himself found in nature and the Bible leaves all mankind guilty before His throne of judgment but are not efficacious to the salvation of any person. Salvation takes the application of this truth to the heart (soul) of the person by God the Holy Spirit.[15] This is what we call regeneration or the rebirth, where God opens the eyes of a fallen man by the supernatural revelation of the Holy Spirit. But this new heart is not in some spiritual way only, but in a realistic way. We read in the Bible "*And I will give them one heart, and I will put a new*

---

[13] Total depravity is not a reference to the depth of man's fall or meant to state that man is so bad that he cannot get worse. Total depravity speaks to the breadth of the fallen nature of mankind and says that man is corrupt in all of his faculties.

[14] This is known as double predestination or in other words there are two decrees, a decree of life and a decree of death. This is error and Dort correctly states the case in the phrase "because of sin," when referring to why some are condemned to hell. To create a separate decree of reprobation would mean God condemned without cause and thereby the sinner could tell God you made me this way. The Bible says man cannot ask this question, not because it confronts God but because all mankind knows they are guilty already. Paul's comments concerning God choosing whom He wills and that the thing created may not question the created do not set this aside. Paul is pointing out the total sovereignty of God not the fact of the election and how it came about. Thus, God may have mercy on whom He wills is a divine truth but not the details of the election.

[15] Mt. 16:15-18

spirit within you; and I will take the stony heart out of their flesh, and will give them an heart of flesh:"[16]

Why did God do this? God created and does all things for His own glory. In the election God left man the ability to choose in difference to the holy angels whom God reserved in holiness and unable to sin. As scripture testifies, not one man has or ever will of his own accord choose God. It takes the gift of faith that comes from God in regeneration by grace alone. God does not violate this ability of man to choose, but God does so providentially order all things that those whom God has elected are made willing to be willing to serve God alone. The choice then of a free creature to worship God alone makes the glory of God manifest. We might try another wording here; man cannot and will not choose God. With the revelation of God and the operation of the Holy Spirit within man, whereby a heart of stone is exchanged for a heart of flesh, life will make the one so enlightened by God to obey God from love and thanksgiving. The preferred wording here is that God makes the elect willing to be willing. "*For it is God which worketh in you both to will and to do of his good pleasure.*"[17]

God's providential ordering of all things is the reality of life not what the created desires or thinks it should be. Here Paul's admonition to the created questioning God is more appropriately applied. There is not only just one God, this God is a Sovereign God free to act as He chooses in counsel with Himself alone and furthermore, able to do all of His holy will.

Questions

1. By what two means does God reveal Himself to man?

2. What is God's ordering of all things known as?

3. In considering there is only one God, what must we also understand besides the fact there is only one God?

---

[16] Ezekiel 11:19

[17] Php. 2:13

The Belgic Confession of Faith, Article III

The Written Word of God

> We confess that this Word of God was not sent nor delivered by the will of man, but that men spake from God, being moved by the Holy Spirit, as the apostle Peter says; and that afterwards God, from a special care which He has for us and our salvation, commanded His servants, the prophets and apostles, to commit His revealed word to writing; and He Himself wrote with His own finger the two tables of the law. Therefore we call such writings holy and divine Scriptures.[18]

The plenary-verbal inspiration of the Scriptures along with the inerrancy and infallibility of the Scriptures are essential doctrines. By plenary-verbal it is meant the Bible is God breathed and so inspired it is as if God had also written the whole with His own hand as God wrote the two tables of the Law. By plenary it is meant first every single word of the Scriptures and secondly that it applies to all mankind with no exceptions. The Bible is an absolute unchangeable whole, written by God. By verbal or God-breathed the authorship is assigned directly to God and not the human writers whom God chose to transmit the revelation of Himself through.

Some otherwise orthodox and wise Christian scholars have faltered here and allowed this only pertains to the original autographs, or that exact first piece of parchment used by the original human author to transcribe these truths. Perhaps the most important among the American scholars to embrace this terminology concerning the autographs was B. B. Warfield. This error was born during the so-called age of enlightenment and higher criticism. Make no mistake this is an error of the highest order and should not be acceptable to any Christian on the face of the earth. To the knowledge of man not one single scrap of any original manuscript of either the Old or New Testament exists. The appeal is then to nothing and leaves the Christian with no defense of the Scriptures.

---

[18] HC Q19; Q22 - H I. all - D Head I Art 3 - WCF I.2 - WSC Q2; Q3 - WLC Q3;Q4;Q5

As noted by John Calvin so eloquently in the opening chapters of the *Institutes of the Christian Religion* the real testimony of the Bible's authenticity and authority comes from within the text itself and the testimony of the Holy Spirit to the spirit of man. Nonetheless to ascribe the very Word of God to oblivion contradicts the words of Jesus Christ who said not the smallest portion would pass away before the end of the world. God has providentially protected His revealed word, the Bible though the ages. Not to unduly fault a brother and scholar such as Warfield who felt the need to make the concession to the academic and secular world, nonetheless such wording is a cop-out and not to be tolerated in the church.[19]

By inerrant it is meant that there is no error in the Word of God. That is where the Bible speaks of history, science, or any other topic it does not contain error as far as it addresses that topic. Infallible means that God has spoken and every word spoken by God will come to pass in God's time without failure. While not all of the words spoken have been literally fulfilled yet, the majority of the prophetic words have been fulfilled in Christ and all the detractors of God throughout the ages have disclosed not one failure. The Word of God will not fail and the proof is within the text itself where we read that God is able to complete or do all of His holy will. Likewise not one single error of fact has ever been disclosed though the devil and his advocates have most ardently tried to cast doubt on the Word of God from the beginning. In the garden with our first parents we find the first attack of Satan is to cast doubt on what God has said, and that battle continues today.

The only concession God made in revealing His will to man was the use of a human intermediary whom God used to actually put pen to paper to write the Holy Scriptures. Thereby, God condescended to man and used the language and nuances of man's limited ability to make the revelation. However, not one writer wrote of his own accord, but as he was borne along by the Holy Spirit. Some object that this removes man and makes man no more than a tool in the hand of God. So it is! Paul seldom wrote with his own hand according to the Bible and none doubt

---

[19] The Westminster Confession of Faith in chapter one correctly points to those documents we do have in the original languages as being the source of all truth needed in all areas of question or controversy. These ancient manuscripts are known as apographs as opposed to the originals that are referred to as the autographs.

the work of Paul was Paul's, though another actually placed pen to paper. Why then would it seem contrary to practice for God to so dictate what God wanted written?

By nature a divine word would have all of these qualities: God breathed, unaltered or complete in all aspects, contain no errors, and could not fail for the purpose it was intended. Unfortunately because of the darkness of sin that besets all flesh the church has had to add these adjectives or qualifying terms as if God needs a defender. The Holy Spirit will testify to the believer that this is God's Word and that should be sufficient. Share this revelation boldly and without apology. Do not fear the ridicule the evil one will bring to bear through his children of the world. Be prepared then in season and out to proclaim Jesus Christ, the Son of God is Lord of all. Fear not those who can destroy the body, but God who is able to condemn the immortal soul to hell forever. God has spoken, and so it is!

Questions

1. Where did the word of God come from?

2. Why do we call the Bible divine Scriptures?

3. What do we mean by plenary-verbal inspiration?

The Belgic Confession of Faith, Article IV
Canonical Books of the Holy Scripture

We believe that the Holy Scriptures are contained in two books, namely, the Old and the New Testament, which are canonical, against which nothing can be alleged. These are thus named in the Church of God.

The books of the Old Testament are the five books of Moses, to wit: Genesis, Exodus, Leviticus, Numbers, Deuteronomy; the book of Joshua, Judges, Ruth, the two books of Samuel, the two of the Kings, two books of the Chronicles, [commonly called Paralipomenon, the first of] Ezra, Nehemiah, Esther; Job, the Psalms [of David], the three books of Solomon, namely, the Proverbs, Ecclesiastes, and the Song of Songs; the four great prophets, Isaiah, Jeremiah, {Lamentations,} Ezekiel, and Daniel; and the twelve lesser prophets, namely, Hosea, Joel, Amos, Obadiah, Jonah, Micah, Nahum, Habakkuk, Zephaniah, Haggai, Zechariah, and Malachi.

Those of the New Testament are the four evangelists, to wit: Matthew, Mark, Luke, and John; the Acts of the Apostles; the thirteen[20] epistles of the apostle Paul, namely, one to the Romans, two to the Corinthians, one to the Galatians, one to the Ephesians, one to the Philippians, one to the Colossians, two to the Thessalonians, two to Timothy, one to Titus, one to Philemon; Hebrews; the seven epistles of the other apostles, namely, one of James, two of

---

[20] 1. "Fourteen" has been changed to "thirteen".
The footnote concerning the change of 14 to 13 is derived from the fact some scholars debate that Paul is the writer of Hebrews. The early fathers appear to name Paul and we have some scholars who continue to credit Paul with this epistle. This is of no real significance in that it is part of the canon and recognized by both sides as being of God.

Peter, three of John, one of Jude; and the Revelation of the apostle John.[21]

Having a canon that is clearly defined is important. The Jewish peoples had a canon that they jealously protected from error in transmission. Christ recognized the authenticity of this Jewish canon. Though not in the same sequential order as we currently hold it, the Christian church made no changes to the Old Testament books which were accepted as being canon.

Very early in its history the Christian church found it necessary to list what books were considered to be Scripture in an effort to stop the widespread use of spurious books claiming to have the authority of Scripture. We find lists of canonical books as early as c. 200. There was some debate through the centuries concerning some books that eventually were accepted by the church as Scripture. There was also some minor controversy concerning the Old Testament, particularly the Song of Solomon.

During the sixteenth century reformation the reformers found it necessary to close the Canon and to specifically exclude those books we now call the Apocrypha. As the controversy over the theology and policies of the Roman Catholic Church grew, Rome found it necessary to recognize the Apocrypha as Canon to validate her beliefs. While the criteria to determine what was Canon used by the reformers was essentially that of the church from the beginning, Rome ignored its own criteria in adding these books to the Bible that church still recognizes today. This made it necessary to list the books in the Canon by name and to declare that the revelation of God concerning the Canon had ended. Some mistakenly think the reformers and particularly the Westminster Assembly thereby declared God no longer communicated with His people in any way outside the Holy Spirit speaking in the Bible.

Make no mistake the Canon[22] is closed. However God does continue to speak and interact with His people. Scripture and the Westminster Confession of Faith both call for believers to test the spirits to see if they are of God. If God no longer communicates

---

[21] HC Q98 - H I all - D Head II Art 5; Head III & IV Art 8;17 - WCF I all - WLC Q5

[22] In place the word "Canon" is intentionally capitalized because it is a substitute for the word Bible. Canon simply means a defined and uniform set of laws.

with His people there would be no need to test any spirit. All admit that there is a subjective element when they demand that the Holy Spirit speaking in Scripture is the only way for man to properly understand and apply the Scripture. However, this subjective element cannot be tested easily according to some and is suspect at best. Communication does not have to be revelation as if the Canon could be changed or added to. Here is the fear of those who demand an end to all communication by God other than the Holy Spirit speaking in Scripture.

Some believe that if God continued to speak to His people that it would mean the Canon is not closed or that we must create a secondary level of revelation by God that was not equal to Scripture. The error is in not seeing that a secondary level of communication has always existed. The apostle John said that not all of the acts and words of Christ was recorded in the Bible. All of the words spoken with authority by the apostles are not recorded. If some words of Christ Himself are not Canon, why would it be necessary to do so with a modern day illumination from God?[23]

The error is founded on one passage of Scripture, Hebrews 1:1-2. This passage does not limit God and say God will never again use one of the former methods. It says God has spoken by a more perfect word, His Son, Jesus Christ. The final appeal is to 1 Cor. 13:10 where it is recorded that when that which is perfect has come, that which is in part will be done away. Consider if this means the incarnation of Christ and His first coming, then we would have no New Testament as this record was written several years to decades after Christ had ascended into heaven. This verse is a reference to the second coming when as Christ said the Word of God meaning the Bible would cease. This can be seen when we compare Mt. 5:18 to 1 Cor. 13:10.[24]

This in no way lessens the Scriptures as being our only guide

---

[23] Perhaps if we were more careful to separate revelation from enlightenment this problem would be dismissed. Great care is indeed the order of the day here as man seems to always move to the extreme edges of all things. SO while no new revelation meaning Scripture is true, it does not mean the Holy Spirit does not severally move as He wills in "speaking" or illuminating the minds of believers.

[24] What rational being would stake his life on an imperfect or incomplete word? The Canon (Bible) is complete and will not be added to or taken away from until that which is perfect (Christ) has come. This is a clear and definite reference to the end of the word or end time.

for faith and practice, it admits a God who is involved with His creation on a continuing basis and gives weight to the promise of God that God will guide His people in a realistic and tangible way.[25] Significant here is the fact that the Bible is a closed canon that cannot be changed, subtracted from, or added to. It is a complete and divine word that is without error and cannot fail to accomplish the full will of God. Debates among men will not change this, and to hold either side of the means by which God communicates with His people should not be a mark of orthodoxy.

Questions

1. Why is it important that we have a canon?

2. What does the Confession mean when it says nothing can be alleged against the Scriptures?

3. Why is it important to believe the Bible is without error and cannot fail in anything it says?

4. What is our only guide of faith and practice?

---

[25] Isa. 30:21

The Belgic Confession of Faith, Article V

Whence the Holy Scriptures Derive Their Dignity and Authority

> We receive all these books, and these only, as holy and canonical, for the regulation, foundation, and confirmation of our faith; believing without any doubt all things contained in them, not so much because the Church receives and approves them as such, but more especially because the Holy Spirit witnesses in our hearts that they are from God, and also because they carry the evidence thereof in themselves. For the very blind are able to perceive that the things foretold in them are being fulfilled.[26]

This is another statement that effectively closes the canon of the Bible and limits it to the sixty-six books previously named. Since the Bible is the only reliable and true source concerning God and His will, the statement that it is upon these books alone the foundation of the church is built and regulated is here extended to the individual believer. Since the Scriptures are those that speak of Christ to say we believe without doubt requires faith since none can believe that Jesus Christ is the Son of God unless the Holy Spirit reveals it as Paul affirms in his epistle to the church at Corinth. What we today define as infallible and inerrant the Belgic Confession simply states we believe all things in these books.

The Roman Catholic Church still affirms that the Bible receives its authority from the church, which revealed it as Scripture and in some places has claimed the authorship of the Bible. This is contrary to the Bible itself and has always been denied by the Reformed churches. The authority of the Bible is within the Bible and it receives authority with the individual by the testimony of the Holy Spirit with the spirit of the believer. Believers, individual and corporately compose the body of Christ. The message of God is to the whole covenant family but has always focused on the individual soul and its relationship to God.

---

[26] H II.1 - D Head III & IV Art 17 - WCF 1 all

The authority of Scripture is then from God and received by man not because the church has said, "Thus saith the Lord" but because God the Holy Spirit says to the believer, this is truth. The appeal to fulfill and continuing fulfillment of prophecy is unique to the Belgic Confession. This is both an objective standard in the prophecies that have been fulfilled and a subjective tool in that continuing unfolding of prophecy is subject to interpretation and the events known to the individual as fact in the flesh. However this is not a distraction in that the Bible is both factual and objective as proven in history and subjective as the individual is able to discern the voice of the Holy Spirit testifying to his spirit.

The heart of the proof however is objective in that all that God has said has been proven truth with the passage of time and the unfolding history of man exactly as foretold in the Bible. Not one single word of prophecy in the Bible that has come to pass has been proven to be in error in the slightest detail. This gives the believer an anchor in a world of uncertainty. God has provided His own Word so the believer can know and practice solid and established doctrine as the only rule of his faith and practice.

All this said, the church has not ignored the voices of the fathers and has used what the church said concerning the individual books of the Bible as one of the marks to determine what is canon and what is not. However the tradition of man is never to be taken above what the revealed Word of God clearly establishes. When the individual or church finds itself in uncharted waters where the fathers of the faith dared not go or went in another direction they should use the utmost care before changing existing tradition or establishing new doctrines. The communion of saints means every believer has the same access to the very mind of Christ as the Holy Spirit speaks from Scripture and will come down at the same place or close enough to agreement that small details are a thing indifferent and should not cause division within the body. The Bible was not established in a vacuum, but duly considered the opinions of all the saints who went before the generation of reformers that declared this is the complete revelation of God, and it may not be deleted from, added to, or changed.

The age of the tradition or the era of the church fathers in the they lived closer to the time of the revelation does not mean it is correct or that a particular father was without error. Every believer today has the same ability to reach the clear conclusion of what God has said as the ancients. Each generation then is bound to examine the traditions of the church in light of the Bible and reform where necessary to conform to the clear teaching of the Bible. This will not uncover anything new, but bring to perfection or maturity God's will for each generation.

Questions

1. How do we know the Bible is true?

2. Where do we find the evidence that the Bible is true?

3. What does the Confession say will let even the blind see the Bible is true?

The Belgic Confession of Faith, Article VI

The Difference Between the Canonical and Apocryphal Books

We distinguish those sacred books from the apocryphal, viz: the third and fourth books of Esdras, the books of Tobit, Judith, Wisdom, Jesus Sirach, Baruch, the Appendix to the book of Esther, the Song of the Three Children in the Furnace, the History of Susannah, of Bel and the Dragon, the Prayer of Manasseh, and the two books of the Maccabees. All of which the Church may read and take instruction from, so far as they agree with the canonical books; but they are far from having such power and efficacy that we may from their testimony confirm any point of faith or of the Christian religion; much less may they be used to detract from the authority of the other, that is, the sacred books.[27]

We considered this topic briefly in the introduction to the Bible and the deliberate exclusion of all other books other than the sixty-six named in the Confession. There was a process used long before the author of the Belgic Confession put pen to paper to decide what was in the Bible. It has never been concealed that other works of equal or greater age existed. It is denied they ever were of God and intended to be in the Bible.

What a farce that today we still see those who speak of the Lost Books of the Bible. Satan never rests, and the lie continues. The Bible is complete under the protection of God Himself, and there is not one word God intended to be in the Bible that is excluded. Thus these books do exist, they however are not Scripture. They can be interesting reading, and perhaps here and there a jewel of understanding of the culture or history of the Bible extracted that helps a person understand the intent of God in certain places within the Holy Bible. Nonetheless, they are not canon as so aptly spoken in this paragraph of the Belgic Confession. Above all, listen to none who claim to have found lost or unknown books or any other word that is equal to the

[27] H I.9 - WCF I.3; 10 - D Head V .14

Bible as received by the Reformed church from her birth and the universal church before that. The one who says the Bible is the Word of God, but needs anything other than God the Holy Spirit to provide illumination is a false prophet and to be resisted by all means available. Two well known sects fit this description today: The Jehovah's Witness, and the Mormon Church, each require their own writings in addition to the Scriptures to obtain God's light for life and eternity.

The Belgic Confession c. 1561 is in agreement with all Reformed Confessions. The Second Helvetic Confession c. 1566 helps us see the conclusion was well established very early in the Reformed churches and was held by other confessions and catechisms that followed these pioneers. The First Helvetic c. 1536 which only differed significantly in regards to the wording concerning the real presence of Christ in the Supper was an attempt to solidify the beliefs of the reformers. The Second Helvetic was written with a background of the completion and publication of Calvin's Institutes, however the earlier confessions standing in essential agreement help us understand these were all concerns of the reformers from day one and not a result of later theologians to introduce new concepts or add their own flavor to the reformation and especially not additions to counter the counter-reformation of the Council of Trent.

The reformation was well on its way when God used Martin Luther to set an official point in time with his Ninety-five Theses. There was much dissent with Rome and her practices before Luther, Calvin, Bullinger and Guido de Bres (the chief author of the Belgic Confession) began their public ministries. The Belgic was primarily a Dutch confession and the Helvetic was Swiss (German) thus we see very early that even under heavy persecution the reformation was essentially throughout continental Europe. This does not claim all these men worked in isolation, but that they worked toward a unified concept of what the true church should be in accordance with the Bible. They were known to each other and many were in regular correspondence with each other during the era of the first reformation.

Questions

1. Do we have the entire Bible now?

2. What may we do with the books of the Apocrypha or for

that matter all works of a religious nature outside the Bible?

3. What was one of the primary concerns of the 16th century reformers concerning the Scriptures?

The Belgic Confession of Faith, Article VII

The Sufficiency of the Holy Scriptures to Be the Only Rule of Faith

We believe that those Holy Scriptures fully contain the will of God, and that whatsoever man ought to believe unto salvation is sufficiently taught therein. For since the whole manner of worship which God requires of us is written in them at large, it is unlawful for any one, though an apostle, to teach otherwise than we are now taught in the Holy Scriptures: nay, though it were an angel from heaven, as the apostle Paul says. For since it is forbidden to add unto or take away anything from the Word of God, it does thereby evidently appear that the doctrine thereof is most perfect and complete in all respects.

Neither may we consider any writings of men, however holy these men may have been, of equal value with those divine Scriptures, nor ought we to consider custom, or the great multitude, or antiquity, or succession of times and persons, or councils, decrees or statutes, as of equal value with the truth of God, since the truth is above all; for all men are of themselves liars, and more vain than vanity itself. Therefore we reject with all our hearts whatsoever does not agree with this infallible rule, as the apostles have taught us, saying, Prove the spirits, whether they are of God. Likewise: If any one cometh unto you, and bringeth not this teaching, receive him not into your house.[28]

A direct rejection of Roman Catholic practice of considering the word of the Roman Pope to be infallible and equal to the Bible being charitable, for in practice if not uniformly by testimony of her clergy today, the Roman Church has always held the word of the Pope to be of all authority. This was one of the prime divisions in the Reformation along with many excesses this

---

[28] H II. 1; 2;3 ;4 - D Head V Art 14 - WCF I. 8;9

heresy allowed to devour Christianity prior to the reformation of the sixteenth century. It stands as a complete blockade of reconciliation of the Protestant churches and Rome today, along with numerous other practices that are idolatry. Rome has not changed or recanted from since the reformation leaving no path to unity with Rome. Yet, Rome's liberal and inclusive false Gospel attracts many blinded by Satan in the name of unity in the Spirit to wander into the Roman graveyard. The attraction to her antiquity and traditions is all compelling to all but the very elect whom the Bible says cannot ultimately be deceived.

As noted in the Confession, the claims of direct succession of office have no weight whatsoever in establishing the pope or the church above the Scriptures. Rome has claimed Peter as their first Pope, a fact that history and the Bible render impossible, and that all succeeding popes are in direct succession to office from the apostles. Even if this were true, it is of no weight since the Bible says that any person; to include a holy angel may not change or set aside the Word of God. Christ said not one jot would pass away from the Bible before the end of the world. God has spoken, and that clearly. This is not debatable nor can a compromise be reached. The true church can have no part of these foul doctrines from hell.

Let all who then see differently turn to the only source of truth and see their error. Movements such as Evangelicals and Catholics Together are dead wrong and trample the martyrs of the reformation under their feet in their haste to believe the lie of Satan. The necessity of the reformation of the sixteenth century is proven by the word and practice of Rome in contradiction of Scripture before and since those defenders of truth laid down their lives in the name of Christ for the purity of Christ's church. Nothing has changed.

Questions

1. Where may we find the full will of God?

2. Who may teach contrary to the Bible and be accepted as teaching the truth?

3. According to the Confession what is above all?

The Belgic Confession of Faith, Article VIII

God Is One in Essence, Yet Distinguished in Three Persons.

According to this truth and this Word of God, we believe in one only God, who is the one single essence, in which are three persons, really, truly, and eternally distinct according to their incommunicable properties; namely, the Father, and the Son, and the Holy Spirit. The Father is the cause, origin, and beginning of all things visible and invisible; the Son is the word, wisdom, and image of the Father; the Holy Spirit is the eternal power and might, proceeding from the Father and the Son. Nevertheless, God is not by this distinction divided into three, since the Holy Scriptures teach us that the Father, and the Son, and the Holy Spirit have each His personality, distinguished by Their properties; but in such wise that these three persons are but one only God.

Hence, then, it is evident that the Father is not the Son, nor the Son the Father, and likewise the Holy Spirit is neither the Father nor the Son. Nevertheless, these persons thus distinguished are not divided, nor intermixed; for the Father has not assumed the flesh, nor has the Holy Spirit, but the Son only. The Father has never been without His Son, or without His Holy Spirit because they are all three co-eternal and co-essential. There is neither first nor last; for they are all three one, in truth, in power, in goodness, and in mercy.[29]

The Trinity defies mere human wisdom, words, or even analogies to define and explain it. Every analogy fails miserably because there is nothing known to man that can be three distinct parts, yet of one essence. For example most have heard the Trinity explained using water because water can be liquid, solid, or gas. The truth here is not that they are three yet one, but they are three

---

[29] HC Q24; Q25 - H III.3; 4; 5 - WCF II.3 - WSC Q6 - WLC Q9; Q10

yet one that cannot be divided in any way. Water is a chemical compound of hydrogen and oxygen it can be divided. Neither does the ability to be in three forms explain anything because the Trinity is always spirit and not distinguished by mode, which in this analogy depends on external circumstance, the temperature. Modalism is the attempt to define the persons of the Trinity by their operations as revealed to man or the "mode." This is heresy in that it denies each is a complete and separate person.

Calvin used the wording one substance or essence and three subsistencies.[30] This is much closer and perhaps as close as we can get in human terms. Subsistence is a reference to the base and essential property (essence) of a substance. It can be seen then as being the essential of existence. Thus we have three subsistencies but one essence.

Later Confessions will use wording such as the Father ever existing, the Son eternally begotten of the Father and the Holy Spirit eternally proceeding from the Father and Son. This isn't a bad way to try and view the Trinity. The metaphysical and esoteric nature of the Trinity leaves it just outside the reach of man to explain in more concrete terms. However, God is spirit and spirit cannot be seen, touched, or tasted by man.[31]

As noted all three are properly God and are co-equal in all things pertaining to the Godhead. This equality however does not as some teach; prohibit any subordination in the Godhead. We see subordination of Son to Father several places in the New Testament when Christ defers to the Father as an example, "Thy will be done." Neither the Son nor Holy Spirit accomplish anything that is not in the eternal counsel of God as the Father. This counsel Scripture declares was with none other than God Himself. However the name God would of necessity have included Son and Holy Spirit. We can assign the mode or personalities involved to this subordination and not infringe upon the fullness of each being totally and properly God. That is as the operation of each is made manifest to man there is a subordination of Son and Spirit to the will of the Father. The

---

[30] Subsistence declares existence or that all three actually exist and have personality.

[31] We must use care here as this can appear to give a beginning or a point of creation to the son and Holy Spirit. Furthermore it implies a subordination of person in the Godhead that does not exist. Subordination within the Godhead is of a voluntary nature such as Christ considering it not robbery to be equal with God, yet obeyed God even to the cross.

care here is not to rob either of their place as being fully God and yet attempt to understand how They can operate as three Persons and not break apart the unity of essence that is all three Persons.

If you don't understand this you are not alone, welcome to the club. God never bothered to explain Himself, just that He existed. The only knowledge man can have about God is that which God reveals about Himself. We then find that we can best explain God by His attributes. Be careful and do not separate God because different attributes appear to be assigned to each Person within the Trinity (see Modalism above). A good example of this is seen in the choice of words used here in the Belgic Confession where it could be understood as some ancient heretics did that the Holy Spirit is nothing more than the power of God and not of the same substance or essence. The Confession isn't in error here, but the wording can be seen as careless by this generation. From the whole we know this was not the intent and the author would have avoided any such wording if he thought it could be misunderstood. This particular terminology was not repeated in later Confessions (The Westminster for example). Likewise, it would appear from the terminology here that a mode of operation is used to prove the Three have never assumed the mode of the other. A presentation that leaves room then for the error of Modalism to spring forth, which is one of the errors, the Confession is expressly trying to refute. Our best theologians over the centuries after struggling with the terminology have for the most part laid aside such attempts and called it an area left within the mystery of God and accepted by faith.

One of my first year professors used a common diagram of a triangle with each person of the Godhead assigned to one of the points of the triangle, then explained that there was no place to view the triangle from outside the triangle where you could ever see more than two Persons of the Godhead. Yet from within the triangle all three can be seen and each at their own point of the complete triangle. The view from within the triangle is the view of a believer. This is an attempt as another way of showing that you can only see the Trinity by faith.

The important things to remember are that all three are totally and properly fully God. The three are equal in all things and all existed from eternity without beginning. The three cannot be divided in essence in any way whatsoever and remain God. While attributes can be distinguished in places, all three are one and their mode of operation does not lessen the power or equality of any. Within the mode of operations we do see a natural subordination, but not of person or equality of the essential essence. Hear O' Israel, the LORD your GOD is One, stands fast as the way God revealed Himself to man. From the very beginning God is spoken of in the Bible in the plural and in the New Testament the doctrine of the Persons within the Godhead becomes clear but never is the word Trinity used to explain this three in one God of Christianity. Three distinct and separate Persons, co-equal in all things, yet one God is what God has revealed and it is true. Faith is substance of things hoped for and the essence of things unseen. To the believer God has spoken and thus it is. To the unbeliever belong the pitiful human attempts to reveal more of God than God has revealed of Himself.

Questions

1. Why do we teach that God is three distinct Persons?

2. What do we mean by co-eternal and co-essential?

3. Even though He is three distinct Persons, why do we say God is cannot be divided?

The Belgic Confession of Faith, Article IX

The Proof of the Foregoing Article of the Trinity of Persons in One God

All this we know as well from the testimonies of Holy Writ as from their operations, and chiefly by those we feel in ourselves. The testimonies of the Holy Scriptures that teach us to believe this Holy Trinity are written in many places of the Old Testament, which are not so necessary to enumerate as to choose them out with discretion and judgment.

In Genesis, chap. 1:26, 27, God says: Let us make man in our image, after our likeness, etc. And God created man in his own image, male and female created he them. And Gen. 3:22, Behold, the man is become as one of us. From this saying, Let us make man in our image, it appears that there are more persons than one in the Godhead; and when He says, God created, He signifies the unity. It is true, He does not say how many persons there are, but that which appears to us somewhat obscure in the Old Testament is very plain in the New. For when our Lord was baptized in Jordan, the voice of the Father was heard, saying, This is my beloved Son; the Son was seen in the water, and the Holy Spirit appeared in the shape of a dove. This form is also instituted by Christ in the baptism of all believers: Make disciples of all the nations, baptizing them into the name of the Father and of the Son and of the Holy Spirit. In the Gospel of Luke the angel Gabriel thus addressed Mary, the mother of our Lord: The Holy Spirit shall come upon thee, and the power of the Most High shall overshadow thee; wherefore also the holy thing which is begotten shall be called the Son of God. Likewise: The grace of the Lord Jesus Christ, and the love of God, and the communion of the Holy Spirit, be with you all. And (A.V.): There are three that bear record in heaven, the Father, the Word, and the Holy Ghost: and these three are one.

In all these places we are fully taught that there are three persons in one only divine essence. And although this doctrine far surpasses all human understanding, nevertheless we now believe it by means of the Word of God, but expect hereafter to enjoy the perfect knowledge and benefit thereof in heaven.

Moreover, we must observe the particular offices and operations of these three persons towards us. The Father is called our Creator, by His power; the Son is our Savior and Redeemer, by His blood; the Holy Spirit is our Sanctifier, by His dwelling in our hearts.

This doctrine of the Holy Trinity has always been affirmed and maintained by the true Church since the time of the apostles to this very day against the Jews, Mohammedans, and some false Christians and heretics, as Marcion, Manes, Praxeas, Sabellius, Samosatenus, Arius, and such like, who have been justly condemned by the orthodox fathers. Therefore, in this point, we do willingly receive the three creeds, namely, that of the Apostles, of Nicea, and of Athanasius; likewise that which, conformable thereunto, is agreed upon by the ancient fathers.[32]

As noted before, the word Trinity is not in the Bible, but the doctrine is clear from both Testaments and has been part of the Christian church from her birth. The error of all the different persons, sects, and men listed above were concerning the doctrine of the Trinity in equality of essence, distinction of person, inviolate unity of person by any means whatsoever. All the heresies of the ancient and present world are founded on an incomplete or wrong Christology.

It is beyond the scope of this work, but to take the time and study the various false doctrines taught by the men and groups

---

[32] H III.5

listed here is worthwhile. There are no new heresies but old error given a new name and run up the flagpole to see who will salute. For example, the current debate about a new doctrine called Open Theism is nothing but an age-old error named for its author Pelagius. While the center of this new error is the autonomy of man, the error ends in a denial of Christ as the only Mediator. Thus, we see a return to violation of the Godhead and a false Christology. We should know and recognize the lies of Satan from the past less such present and future attempts by the devil detract the attention of the church from her appointed duty of gathering and perfecting the saints that all the world might be taught whatsoever God has commanded.

Denial of the Trinity is denial of God in that Paul notes that God has personally revealed to those who do not have the Scriptures the power and mystery of the Godhead. By Godhead Paul is speaking of the Trinity (Rom 1:20). There is no excuse for the debate and confusion many would place around or attempt to cover the doctrine of the Trinity in or with. However, the doctrine of the Trinity is of such importance we see the fathers of the Reformation take the time to show the logic and reasoning of Scripture to prove the doctrine in one of the longer articles of this confession.

Questions

1. When in church history was the doctrine of the Trinity formed?

2. As we consider the Trinity how many distinct offices do we find in the Bible?

3. The doctrine of the Trinity being beyond mortal understanding, how can we believe it is true?

The Belgic Confession of Faith, Article X
Jesus Christ Is True and Eternal God

We believe that Jesus Christ according to His divine nature is the only begotten Son of God, begotten from eternity, not made, nor created (for then He would be a creature), but co-essential and co-eternal with the Father, the very image of his substance and the effulgence of his glory, equal unto Him in all things. He is the Son of God, not only from the time that He assumed our nature but from all eternity, as these testimonies, when compared together, teach us. Moses says that God created the world; and St. John says that that Word which he calls God made all things. The apostle says that God made the world by His Son; likewise, that God created all things by Jesus Christ. Therefore it must needs follow that He who is called God, the Word, the Son, and Jesus Christ, did exist at that time when all things were created by Him. Therefore the prophet Micah says: His goings forth are from of old, from everlasting. And the apostle: He hath neither beginning of days nor end of life. He therefore is that true, eternal, and almighty God whom we invoke, worship, and serve.[33]

Jesus Christ is the Son of God! Remove the deity of Christ and you have defeated God as if that can be done. Nonetheless, all world religions outside Christianity attempt to remove the cloak of divinity from Christ. If it can be proven Christ is not God, fully in all regards and co-equal to God, then there is no atonement and the Bible is a myth of no more value than any other literature of man. If Christ can be proven to have a beginning either in the incarnation or before, then the foundation of the Christian church is shattered. Christ declared that upon His deity he founded the church and the gates of hell would not prevail against the church. Nonetheless, we see the attack of Satan and his earthly kingdom begin by casting doubt on the Word of God where the deity of

---

[33] HC Q17; Q18; Q33 - H XI.1; 2; 3 - D Head II Art 4 - WCF VIII.2 - WSC Q21 - WLC Q11; Q36; Q38; Q40

Christ is revealed. Defeat the veracity of Scripture and you remove Christ and there is no church. This is why we see our theologians from the beginning not argue so much the existence of God as that God has spoken and we have the exact record of those things, which God commanded. The Word of God alone has the authority or ability to reveal Christ as the Son of God eternally existing and eternally begotten of the Father without beginning or end. The only source of absolute truth is the Word of God.

Questions

1. There are several things Christ is said to be co-eternal with the Father in; name two.

2. What two verses of Scripture may we compare to show that Christ has always existed?

3. Which Old Testament prophet testified to the eternal nature of Christ?

The Belgic Confession of Faith, Article XI
The Holy Spirit Is True and Eternal God

We believe and confess also that the Holy Spirit from eternity proceeds from the Father and the Son; and therefore neither is made, created, nor begotten, but only proceeds from both; who in order is the third person of the Holy Trinity; of one and the same essence, majesty, and glory with the Father and the Son; and therefore is the true and eternal God, as the Holy Scriptures teach us.[34]

This is the third person of the Trinity, the Godhead spoken of by Paul in Romans one. While each has personal attributes, characteristics, and is distinct, all three are one God. They are of one essence yet three subsistencies to use Calvin's term, which is the best way to explain the three yet, one Person of God. The reformed formulation has always been that it is proper for the Father to eternally exist and the Son to be eternally begotten of the Father, and the Holy Sprit to be eternally proceeding from Father and Son.

Remember the caution concerning divisions of any kind whatsoever from previous articles. Also watch out for the easiest heresy to enter, that of Modalism. We do not have a Father of wrath, a Loving Son, and a gift bearing Spirit, we have one God made manifest in three distinct and separate Persons, yet of one essential substance. In this sense the words of Christ that if you have seen Him you have seen the Father can be said of the Holy Spirit and it isn't wrong to say where one Person is the other three are present by necessity because these three are one. Don't try to understand it perfectly, receive the truth of the Bible by faith and cling tight to its eternal truth. This brings up the last point that is crucial, the formulation above by our reformed forefathers uses the word eternally with all three Persons so there can be no confusion that all three are properly God and do not have a beginning or end.

Questions

---

[34] HC Q53 - WLC Q11

1. How do we describe the eternal nature of the Holy Spirit in relationship to the Godhead?

2. What attributes of God does the [C]confession use in this article to show the eternal nature of the Holy Spirit?

3. Where do we learn the truth concerning the Holy Spirit?

The Belgic Confession of Faith, Article XII

The Creation of All Things, Especially the Angels

We believe that the Father by the Word, that is, by His Son, has created of nothing the heaven, the earth, and all creatures, when it seemed good unto Him; giving unto every creature its being, shape, form, and several offices to serve its Creator; that He also still upholds and governs them by His eternal providence and infinite power for the service of mankind, to the end that man may serve his God.

He also created the angels good, to be His messengers and to serve His elect; some of whom are fallen from that excellency in which God created them into everlasting perdition, and the others have by the grace of God remained steadfast and continued in their first state. The devils and evil spirits are so depraved that they are enemies of God and every good thing; to the utmost of their power as murderers watching to ruin the Church and every member thereof, and by their wicked stratagems to destroy all; and are, therefore, by their own wickedness adjudged to eternal damnation, daily expecting their horrible torments.

Therefore we reject and abhor the error of the Sadducees, who deny the existence of spirits and angels; and also that of the Manichees, who assert that the devils have their origin of themselves, and that they are wicked of their own nature, without having been corrupted.[35]

God created all things that exist out of nothing by the power of His word alone. From the plurality of the terms used and from the Scripture as rendered by the pen of John we can see the Son as the Word was present and was also the Creator. Likewise we see the presence of the Holy Spirit in the creation account. Not

---

[35] HC Q6 - H VII all - WCF IV.1;2 - WSC Q9; Q10 - WLC Q15; Q16; Q17

addressed here in the Belgic Confession and space doesn't permit a proper treatment, but God created all in the space of six literal 24 hours and the so called frame-work hypotheses is pure bunk and though accepted in some Reformed circles is gross error if not heresy and is not to be embraced by the saints of God.

God created the angels of heaven good, as all things created by God were good by God's own declaration. Yet like man God permitted some to fall, the rest in grace preserving eternally in righteousness to the point that they are called holy angels. One third of the angels fell in the sin of Satan and were cast out of heaven. There is one devil in the sense this is usually reserved for Satan himself, but in a sense all fallen angels are devils. So called evil spirits and devils are all fallen angels as God did not create evil creatures as such, but the will of the creature led them into all evil and in total warfare against God for all eternity. Human spirits do not wander the earth and all spiritual presences are of God or of these fallen angels. Thus the Bible tells us to test the spirits because fallen angels were once angels of light and are spiritual beings capable in making themselves manifest in diverse ways and forms even as the holy angels are.

The Bible is clear that these spiritual beings exist and to deny such is to deny the very Word of God and all saints should condemn as heresy any belief that denies the truth of God's revealed Word. Nothing of any substance whatsoever, visible or invisible to the created was created from nothing and nothing exists which was not created by God. The devils are fallen angels as the Bible says and not of their own making but of the Creation of God and created good. Their sinful condition was of themselves, not their creation.

Questions

1. How does God continue to order and sustain all things?

2. For what purpose were angels created?

3. What was the error of the Sadducees?

The Belgic Confession of Faith, Article XIII
The Providence of God and His Government of All Things

We believe that the same good God, after He had created all things, did not forsake them or give them up to fortune or chance, but that He rules and governs them according to His holy will, so that nothing happens in this world without His appointment; nevertheless, God neither is the Author of nor can be charged with the sins which are committed. For His power and goodness are so great and incomprehensible that He orders and executes His work in the most excellent and just manner, even then when devils and wicked men act unjustly. And as to what He does surpassing human understanding, we will not curiously inquire into farther than our capacity will admit of; but with the greatest humility and reverence adore the righteous judgments of God, which are hid from us, contenting ourselves that we are pupils of Christ, to learn only those things which He has revealed to us in His Word, without transgressing these limits.

This doctrine affords us unspeakable consolation, since we are taught thereby that nothing can befall us by chance, but by the direction of our most gracious and heavenly Father; who watches over us with a paternal care, keeping all creatures so under His power that not a hair of our head (for they are all numbered), nor a sparrow can fall to the ground without the will of our Father, in whom we do entirely trust; being persuaded that He so restrains the devil and all our enemies that without His will and permission they cannot hurt us. And therefore we reject that damnable error of the Epicureans, who say that God regards nothing but leaves all things to chance.[36]

---

[36] HC Q26; Q27; Q28; Q125 - H VI all - WCF V all - WSC Q11 - WLC Q18; Q19; Q20

Providence is the doctrine under discussion in this article. It is by providence that God orders all things, even those perceived by man as evil or bad to conform to God's own purpose and to work for the ultimate good of the Elect.

It is necessary to distinguish between decree and providence. There is only one eternal decree, the decree of election to salvation in Jesus Christ. Those who teach a so-called double-predestination violate this article and Scripture and lay sin at the feet of God. If God made a separate and special decree of reprobation, then those God did not elect could not chose God even if they desired to do so. The effect is exactly the same regarding reprobation with one decree to election and a passive action as such whereby God simply passes by the non-elect.

This article correctly cautions trying to see behind the mystery of God where we cannot go. However even the flawed logic of fallen man can penetrate the perfect and revealed will of God enough to see the necessity of this statement. The problem for man is that of time or history. God is not within time, which God created for the benefit of man. God is ever present and sees the end from the beginning. The Reformed have always been careful to insist that God did not use divine foresight in the election or it would introduce the element of works or merit and negate grace. If we first have one eternal decree of election without employing divine foresight, then the use of providence to order all things for the good of the elect does not leave sin at the feet of God so to speak and thus Scripture is true when it says God created evil, for God created all things, yet sin is not of God but the ability to sin God left with the created to include the elect. This introduces the bias between the infra/supra-lapsarians.

The Synod of Dort uses the phrase because of sin, which many use to claim God decreed the fall and then elected. I disagree, God knew man would fall and foreordained that event, but elected without regard to the fall as such. There is a difference between foreordain (providence) and election. The decree of a sovereign cannot be broken or changed (Consider the actions of an earthly sovereign in the story of Esther to see the concept of the inability of a ruler to change his mind.) Dort is correct, the election was because of sin, but the election preceded the sin and fall in the eternal counsel of God.

This is an important concept and is where God permits man

to pray and for God to answer that prayer, yet God doesn't change His mind, having foreordained everything from the beginning. If everything were predestinated, as some are want to present foreordination, then Hezekiah would not have received 15 more years to live. God is in absolute control and all things great or small are so ordered to bring about God's perfect will. In other words as here noted there are no accidents, we do not live at the whim of chance or a so-called fate, but in the will of God the Father from the beginning.

Can we go here? To a certain decree we can see within the eternal counsel by the use of God-given abilities. However this has never been the measure of orthodoxy in the Reformed churches because it is an area of shadow and not clearly presented in the Bible. Thus, infra and supra are not a litmus test and can co-exist even in the same congregation. What cannot be violated is the sovereignty of God and the idea God doesn't remain active in His creation and so orders earthly events in accord with His perfect will and the good of the elect.

Here we indeed have much comfort for we know that nothing whatsoever can happen to us without the permission of God and therefore even those things that will drive the unbeliever farther from God will draw the saint in adversity toward God. Here is the comfort and strength needed to live an abundant life despite earthly circumstance. This is the faith that sustained the martyred defenders of truth whereby they could walk into the arena filled with wild beasts with a song on their lips and joy in their hearts. We do not live by experience however, but the Word of God and the just live by faith. Providence is the experience of the Romans 5:1-5 passage that brings forth hope in the heart of the believer.

Questions

1. How does God order and execute His work when devils and wicked men act unjustly?

2. What should we do concerning the things God has kept within His mystery?

3. What can happen to a believer by mere chance?

The Belgic Confession of Faith, Article XIV

The Creation and Fall of Man, and His Incapacity to Perform What Is Truly Good

We believe that God created man out of the dust of the earth, and made and formed him after His own image and likeness, good, righteous, and holy, capable in all things to will agreeably to the will of God. But being in honor, he understood it not, neither knew his excellency, but willfully subjected himself to sin and consequently to death and the curse, giving ear to the words of the devil. For the commandment of life, which he had received, he transgressed; and by sin separated himself from God, who was his true life; having corrupted his whole nature; whereby he made himself liable to corporal and spiritual death. And being thus become wicked, perverse, and corrupt in all his ways, he has lost all his excellent gifts which he had received from God, and retained only small remains thereof, which, however, are sufficient to leave man without excuse; for all the light which is in us is changed into darkness, as the Scriptures teach us, saying: The light shineth in the darkness, and the darkness apprehended it not; where St. John calls men darkness.

Therefore we reject all that is taught repugnant to this concerning the free will of man, since man is but a slave to sin, and can receive nothing, except it have been given him from heaven. For who may presume to boast that he of himself can do any good, since Christ says: No man can come to me, except the Father that sent me draw him? Who will glory in his own will, who understands that the mind of the flesh is enmity against God? Who can speak of his knowledge, since the natural man receiveth not the things of the Spirit of God? In short, who dares suggest any thought, since he knows that we are not sufficient of ourselves to account anything as of ourselves, but that our sufficiency is of God? And therefore what the apostle says ought justly to be held sure and firm, that God worketh in us both to will and to work, for his good pleasure. For there is no understanding nor will conformable to the divine understanding and will but what Christ has wrought in man; which He teaches us, when He says: Apart from me ye can do nothing.[37]

In the image of God is an interesting study. The Bible does not elaborate and thus the fallen mind of man cannot uncover what God has left covered. The best our theologians have done through the ages is to admit man has some of the attributes of God, though in a much less perfection. For example man has reason even as God must have. However the division of the divine attributes into two columns, one consisting of those attributes of God called communicable, or that God passed to man created in His image. The second column contains those attributes that are called incommunicable or that God does not pass along to man created in God's image. For example, God is love and because God first loved man, man has the ability to know love, but not that perfect all consuming love God is or to the degree of perfection of love in God. Since God has chosen to primarily reveal personal knowledge of Himself in the attributes, this is a good place to see what the image of God that remained in man is. It will be broken and perhaps barely discernable, but it is there and as noted here, this light (God is light) remaining is enough to leave sin at the hand of the created and not chargeable to God.

The Reformed have always demanded the complete denial of free will or autonomy of mankind. Simultaneously the Reformed point to the Scriptureas here and say it is of God both for man to will and to do in making this statement. Care must be used here because while it establishes grace and the necessity of the election, it also removes the glory God receives in the election. If God created the inability of the elect to refuse grace (and one of the classic points of Calvinism is irresistible grace) then God has no glory from the created doing what God has foreordained to be, man is a mere robot. The glory of God comes from a free agent willingly serving God in love and obedience. How can both of

---

[37] HC Q5;Q7; Q8; Q9; Q10 - H VIII all - Dort Head I 1; Head II 1;2 - WCF VI all - WSC Q13; Q14; Q15; Q16; Q17; Q18 - WLC Q21; Q22; Q23; Q24; Q25; Q26

these statements be true? God supernaturally reveals Himself to the elect whole leaving the elect in their sin until the elect see that they cannot save themselves and the only truth is God to whom they turn in regeneration by the Holy Spirit. In other words, regeneration enhances the light remaining from the fall so man can see the truth of God. It can be said then that man is free, and at the same time God makes man willing to be willing. Man apart from regeneration will not see the light and continue in the downward spiral away from God. Notice that the holy angels who are prevented from sin glorify God, but it is the worship of mankind that brings glory to God. As Paul said those who heard the Gospel and turned to God by his preaching were his glory, so all believers are the glory of God. This gives no room for man to choose God nor does it make man a mere robot who cannot resist God. Regeneration can be seen as a renewal or enhancement of the light in humanity from being in the image of God. However, it cannot attain perfection in fallen flesh because in the flesh is the will of the creature and the will of the created is evil.

As noted here and by Paul in Romans chapter one, the remaining light is enough so all mankind stands condemned already for not turning to God. Yet, no one single man apart from Christ has ever turned toward God without God's grace and mercy being first bestowed upon that person. Man likes the Gospel as presented in John 3:16, God so loved the world… and tries to ignore the following verses whereby they are condemned already. Man can hear and believe and in the worship of their own imagination retain autonomy is the error of all who do not embrace the truth of Jesus Christ the only way of salvation. It is the error of the Arminian who would leave with man the ability to choose heaven or hell. The Bible says that even the devil believes God exists and trembles at the knowledge. To surrender the will to God in love and obedience thus fulfilling the purpose of creation and the only duty required of man by God will not happen apart from grace in election. So both statements are true, but require each other for the proper understanding.

Questions

1. From what and how was man formed?

2. What do we believe concerning the free will of man?

3. If man is free how does God move man to do His will

without violating that freedom to choose good or evil?

The Belgic Confession of Faith, Article XV
Original Sin

We believe that through the disobedience of Adam original sin is extended to all mankind; which is a corruption of the whole nature and a hereditary disease, wherewith even infants in their mother's womb are infected, and which produces in man all sorts of sin, being in him as a root thereof, and therefore is so vile and abominable in the sight of God that it is sufficient to condemn all mankind. Nor is it altogether abolished or wholly eradicated even by regeneration;[1] since sin always issues forth from this woeful source, as water from a fountain; notwithstanding it is not imputed to the children of God unto condemnation, but by His grace and mercy is forgiven them. Not that they should rest securely in sin, but that a sense of this corruption should make believers often to sigh, desiring to be delivered from this body of death.

Wherefore we reject the error of the Pelagians, who assert that sin proceeds only from imitation.

1.   "Baptism" has been changed to "regeneration"[38].

John in the book of Revelation prays for Christ to come quickly. I doubt many men actually ever pray for God to end the world today, right this minute. Yet this is the position all saints should ever be in before the God of grace who called His own from darkness to light.

God says that He does not punish the children for the sins of the father, yet this appears to be happening when we call for original sin to come from natural generation alone. It also becomes more complex to explain how Christ who was made of a

---

[38] HC Q11; Q12; Q13; Q14 - H VIII all - D Head III & IV 1; 2 ; 34 - WSC Q19 - WLC Q28; Q29

woman did not have the taint of original sin also.

It can be claimed that since the line of inheritance within the Hebrews as the first chosen of God as His people was only through the male, that Christ not having a human father was exempted from the natural generation of the original sin. Or we can use the so-called federal theory whereby Adam as the representative of all men who followed by natural generation and his sin was imputed to all of his posterity. Christ as the second Adam and not being in the generation of Adam because of the virgin birth being sinless had His righteousness imputed to all of the elect. Since God decided the whole in eternity and even the Old Testament saints were saved by faith, God having made the covenant of grace with Christ on behalf of the elect before the foundation of the earth all saints have been saved by the same method. Christ did not begin at His incarnation, but God was made manifest in the incarnation whereby Christ said those who had seen Him had seen God. The correct terminology here is that of federal representation and imputation. The Psalmist declares blessed is the man to whom God does not impute his sins. Imputation means placing in the account of so that God doesn't account the elect sinful, but imputes to the elect the righteousness of Christ, not the sin of Adam.

I prefer imputation as the most consistent way to explain how all are sinful in Adam, yet from the beginning the elect though sinners have not been seen by God as sinners, but righteous. The Westminster Confession says that the Covenant of Grace was made with Christ in behalf of the elect. I see this as the best understanding and it would transcend the dispensation of Old and New Testaments whereas other formulations will fail at one place or another. Thus all mankind as represented in Adam except Christ, who was the new or second Adam, are sinners by natural generation and imputation of their own sins. Thus the Bible declares that man is conceived and born in sin, condemned already.

This returns all to the grace of God, as God in grace does not impute the sins of the elect to the elect, but rather imputes to the elect the righteousness of Christ, which is not theirs by any right and cannot be earned by the performance of any duty whatsoever.

Questions

1. What is the origin of original sin?

2. Does regeneration completely remove from man the corruption of the original sin?

3. Why is this body called the body of death and why would believers want to be free of it?

The Belgic Confession of Faith, Article XVI

Eternal Election

We believe that, all the posterity of Adam being thus fallen into perdition and ruin by the sin of our first parents, God then did manifest Himself such as He is; that is to say, merciful and just: merciful, since He delivers and preserves from this perdition all whom He in His eternal and unchangeable counsel of mere goodness has elected in Christ Jesus our Lord, without any respect to their works; just, in leaving others in the fall and perdition wherein they have involved themselves.[39]

This is a good statement concerning election in that it avoids the pitfall of a so-called double pre-destination. It leaves the question of infra/supra-lapsarianism open, but so does Scripture in many places.

If God had elected any to reprobation before the foundation of the earth, then it could be claimed that they were not guilty of sin in that God had predestined them to sin. As a passive act of passing by in non-election the sin remains at the hand of the created, not God. There is one eternal decree, the decree of election to eternal salvation in Christ of those whom God in counsel with Himself and for His own purpose of His glory alone elected.

There is a difference in a decree and preordained or foreordained. A decree has a forensic element, which demands justice and immutability from a sovereign concerning that decree. If all things were foreordained by decree, men are but robots and there is ultimately no glory to God. Angels glorify God but they are not the glory of God because there is no free ability of the angels not to sin since the original fall. God left with mankind the ability to sin and yet saves some despite their sins. When creatures with the ability to sin and deny God of their own free will worship God, they become God's glory.

---

[39] HC Q54 - H X all - D Head 1 art 6; 7; 9; 10; 11; 12 - WCF III all - WSC Q7; Q8 - WLC Q12; Q13; Q14

The oldest and continuing error in the church concerns the free will of mankind. There seems to be within all of creation the desire for autonomy and the exercise of will. Satan used this natural desire to tempt the first human beings in the garden. There seems to be tremendous difficulty on the part of humankind to understand how man is a free agent yet the elect cannot refuse grace or the non-elect obtain grace, if grace is indeed offered to all. The correct understanding comes from the fact that all mankind is dead in sin and not one single person apart from Christ has ever first sought God. The offer is indeed placed on the table so to speak for all of mankind to partake of. Yet, not one will partake apart from the gift of grace in regeneration and justification in Christ. The Bible says that it is of God for man both to will and to do. This does not violate the free will of man in that in the gift of regeneration man for the first time can see his own fallen condition and imperfection in contrast to a perfect and holy God. Thus the correct Reformed formulation is that God makes man willing to be willing. The calling of man to God through faith in Christ alone requires God to certainly and distinctly to give the gift of faith needed to respond. Thus the free offer is not violated nor is the eternal election and limited atonement negated.

This is a crucial statement that all Reformed must understand. Thus, this statement is well worded, but does need the above understanding so it is properly held in its place of importance in Reformed theology. What man does not understand man is indifferent toward or ignores altogether. The Reformed faith cannot afford either of these luxuries.

As explained before the infra/supra controversy isn't the key here, the result of a free offer to free men, yet all cannot choose the free gift is the issue. Only the Reformed hold this crucial doctrine in the correct bias where the love of God is not in contradiction to the sovereignty and justice of God.

Questions

1. What part did God's foreknowledge play in the election?

2. Why was the election a necessity?

3. Who involves man in sin?

The Belgic Confession of Faith, Article XVII

The Recovery of Fallen Man

> We believe that our most gracious God, in His admirable wisdom and goodness, seeing that man had thus thrown himself into physical and spiritual death and made himself wholly miserable, was pleased to seek and comfort him, when he trembling fled from His presence, promising him that He would give His Son (who would be born of a woman) to bruise the head of the serpent and to make him blessed.[40]

This statement founded firmly on Genesis 3:15 has a very distinct infra-lapsarian inference to it. Thus a non-key theory keeps popping to the surface in the creation, fall, and salvation of man. The problem is because man thinks in a linear fashion, which is one thought at a time in a distinct progression of thought. Whereas, God is outside history or time and all things are before God at all times. God's thoughts are not our thoughts. We need to use care that we do not cause God to change His mind as we formulate our theology at this loci. The immutability of God must not be violated; God cannot change.

The problem is that both infra and supra are references to the eternal counsel of God, before creation. Man cannot go there and it is left in the mystery of God and it is sinful for man to transgress beyond what God has clearly by revealed word or clear inference revealed about Himself. Yet, we must humbly tread here to hold the truth in all of its integrity as revealed by God. It is not sinful therefore to say God elected before the fall in the eternal counsel because all things being before God at all times means God did not and does not have to think in a linear fashion as the created must do. God decided to create knowing that man would fall even as the angels before the creation of man would. God protected the holy angels from sin and saved some sinful men from their own folly by eternal decree before the first word of creation was uttered. This is the key, when did God make the election, in the eternal counsel, not in history. Both infra and supra are in the eternal counsel and not after creation and fall as many understand

---

[40] HC Q12; Q18 - H V.2; 3 - WCF VIII.1

this controversy. Thus this is not an issue to divide the church and is not a measure of orthodoxy. To place the salvation of the elect after creation and the fall is heresy in that it creates a changeable God.[41]

God knew before the first word of creation some angels and all mankind would sin. God preserved some angels in holiness and saved some in Christ before even the angels were created. Sin entered then by the will of the creature, not of God's decree. The irrefutable record of the will of all created, both angels and men to obey their own will over God's will should settle the issue of man being autonomous with the ability to choose God. The will of man is always evil according to Paul who said that because of the always-present evil of the will he did things he hated and did not do what he wanted to do.

Could God have stopped sin from happening in angels and men? That is a silly question, God foreordained all that is or will be. The reason God created all things was for His own glory. To stop the development of sin would have removed all glory from God in the creation. Free agents choosing God and voluntarily obeying God instead of their own will is the glory of God. The election then stands firm, and God through the election and the gift of faith in time, saves some for His own glory. The fact God must overtly act on and in the elect doesn't violate free will, it reveals to the fallen man his foul condition and inability to save himself. So while some find it offensive to use the term choose, the elect do choose God, but it does require the gift of grace in election to turn man toward God. Grace to grace is accurate in that the first grace of election is brought to fruit in the gift of faith by grace.

---

[41] For the sake of clarity here, the reference is to the place in the "sequence" of God's thought in the eternal council. The whole of the controversy depends on how we view God in relation to time or sequence before the creation of all things. To make the decision to elect after the historical fact of creation would be heresy in my mind since it makes God a God of contingency, not a Sovereign, All Knowing, and Ever Present God. It requires Satan to have foiled God's first plan and the election and covenant with Christ is a reaction to that failure.

Questions

1. What two attributes of God played a part in the election?

2. Where do we find the first reference in the Bible to a Savior?

3. What did God say this Savior would make man?

The Belgic Confession of Faith, Article XVIII

The Incarnation of Jesus Christ

We confess, therefore, that God has fulfilled the promise which He made to the fathers by the mouth of His holy prophets, when He sent into the world, at the time appointed by Him, His own only-begotten and eternal Son, who took upon Him the form of a servant and became like unto man, really assuming the true human nature with all its infirmities, sin excepted; being conceived in the womb of the blessed virgin Mary by the power of the Holy Spirit without the means of man; and did not only assume human nature as to the body, but also a true human soul, that He might be a real man. For since the soul was lost as well as the body, it was necessary that He should take both upon Him, to save both.

Therefore we confess (in opposition to the heresy of the Anabaptists, who deny that Christ assumed human flesh of His mother) that Christ partook of the flesh and blood of the children; that He is a fruit of the loins of David after the flesh; born of the seed of David according to the flesh; a fruit of the womb of Mary; born of a woman; a branch of David; a shoot of the root of Jesse; sprung from the tribe of Judah; descended from the Jews according to the flesh; of the seed of Abraham, since (A.V.) he took on him the seed of Abraham, and was made like unto his brethren

in all things, sin excepted; so that in truth He is
our IMMANUEL, that is to say, God with us.[42]

As God pronounced the curse upon all of creation because of
the sin of Adam and Eve, God also opened the mystery of heaven
and promised a Redeemer (Gen. 3:15). From this so-called proto-
evangel in Genesis God proceeds throughout the Bible to
progressively reveal Himself and make the promise clearer until in
God's own time the perfection of God's Word appeared in the
flesh in the incarnation of Jesus Christ. This is best set before us in
the Gospel of John where John begins with this truth of Jesus
Christ as the divine Logos.

This is one of the most crucial doctrines of the church. We
could go so far as to say that if this statement concerning Christ's
birth and the hypostatic union (of the essential essence of) making
Jesus Christ fully man and fully God is not true, then there is no
atonement and God has no chosen people. No other explanation
can fill the righteous requirements of God's judgment and
overcome death, and be accepted by God as fulfillment of all
prophecies. Jesus Christ, fully man and fully God is a mystery not
unlike the Godhead itself and cannot be described by simile or
analogy. As Christ said to Peter, "Flesh and blood has not revealed
this to you…" This truth can only be grasped in faith and this is
why it is written in the Bible that without faith man cannot please
God. Faith is so central we find the exact phrase, "The just shall
live by faith," in the Bible three times.

The Westminster Standards go to some length showing why it
is essential for Jesus Christ to be both God and man united in
eternity. This is one of the doctrines of the church most often
attacked by detractors of the Christian faith. All heresies have at
their root an improper Christology. The Bible is the only source of
perfect truth and the Bible reveals Jesus Christ. Satan's temptation
in the garden thus began by disputing and trying to cast doubt on
the Word of God.

It is also crucial that in the birth of Christ we understand that
this is not the beginning of Christ, but the revelation of God the

---

[42] HC Q35; Q36; Q37; Q38; Q39; Q40 - H XI.4; 5; 9; 10;11; 12; 13; 14; 18 - WCF VIII.4 - WSC Q22; Q27; Q28 - WLC Q37; Q46; Q47; Q48; Q49;Q50; Q51; Q52; Q53; Q54;Q55; Q56; Q57

Son who is without beginning or end. All things are revealed in God's time according to God's divine game plan for the salvation of the elect for His own glory alone.

Without the shedding of blood there is no atonement. Without the perfect sacrifice without blemish there is no atonement. All of which point to the necessity of Jesus Christ and God Himself providing what man cannot provide for himself. Either this statement stands, or Christianity is a mere fantasy and there is no hope for mankind. Yet, the church allows those within her ranks to continue to attack or diminish this key doctrine. It is correctly written that judgment shall begin in the house of God and these so-called scholars and teachers along with the liberal church shall answer to God personally for this blasphemy.

Questions

1. How was Christ conceived?

2. Does Christ have a real soul and a real body?

3. Jesus Christ was the manifestation of what Old Testament hope?

The Belgic Confession of Faith, Article XIX

The Union and Distinction of the Two Natures in the Person of Christ

We believe that by this conception the person of the Son is inseparably united and connected with the human nature; so that there are not two Sons of God, nor two persons, but two natures united in one single person; yet each nature retains its own distinct properties. As, then, the divine nature has always remained uncreated, without beginning of days or end of life, filling heaven and earth, so also has the human nature not lost its properties but remained a creature, having beginning of days, being a finite nature, and retaining all the properties of a real body. And though He has by His resurrection given immortality to the same, nevertheless He has not changed the reality of His human nature; forasmuch as our salvation and resurrection also depend on the reality of His body. But these two natures are so closely united in one person that they were not separated even by His death. Therefore that which He, when dying, commended into the hands of His Father, was a real human spirit, departing from His body. But in the meantime the divine nature always remained united with the human, even when He lay in the grave; and the Godhead did not cease to be in Him, any more than it did when He was an infant, though it did not so clearly manifest itself for a while. Wherefore we confess that He is very God and very man: very God by His power to conquer death; and very man that He might die for us according to the infirmity of His flesh.[43]

This article opens with an explanation of the union of Christ and man we mentioned in the previous article as the hypostatic

---

[43] HC Q15; Q16; Q17 - H XI.6; 7;8 - WCF VIII.2; 3; 7 - WSC Q21 - WLC Q36; Q38; Q39

union. This Confession immediately proceeds to establish the fact Christ is fully God. Likewise, God eternally existing without beginning or end is given to the person of Christ. The Westminster formulation of it being proper for God to eternally exist and for the Son to eternally be begotten of God, and for the Holy Spirit to eternally proceed from Father and Son is written in this manner for this very cause of establishing the eternal existence and co-equality of all three Persons in the Godhead.

In continuing to mention that there was a soul that was at the time of death separated from the body though a Biblical truth is emphasized here to again hold the fully man portion of this doctrine solidly within the Bible. Christ then as the Bible declares becomes the first fruit among many brethren.

The end of this article states a divine truth in human language in that if was only God, then Christ could not die and there is no atonement for it is written that without the shedding of blood there is no atonement. That Christ was fully God is testified to by first the inability of death to hold Christ in its bonds whereby Christ as only God could do defeated death, both physically and spiritually.

Questions

1. We believe there are not two persons but two what in Christ?

2. What is one distinction of the divine nature as opposed to the human nature of Christ?

3. What did Christ commend to God when [H]he died on the cross?

The Belgic Confession of Faith, Article XX

God Has Manifested His Justice and Mercy in Christ

> We believe that God, who is perfectly merciful and just, sent His Son to assume that nature in which the disobedience was committed, to make satisfaction in the same, and to bear the punishment of sin by His most bitter passion and death. God therefore manifested His justice against His Son when He laid our iniquities upon Him, and poured forth His mercy and goodness on us, who were guilty and worthy of damnation, out of mere and perfect love, giving His Son unto death for us, and raising Him for our justification, that through Him we might obtain immortality and life eternal.[44]

The balance of God's love and God's justice is only manifested in Christ and points perfectly to the necessity of Christ being fully man and fully God. Calvin maintained this balance of sovereignty and justice in contrast to God's love and mercy. Luther leaned to the grace and love of God while Zwingli was much more legalistic and focused on the sovereignty of God. We see more of Zwingli's approach in the Westminster documents than other confessions After Calvin and during the so-called enlightenment and age of textural criticism we will not find any single theologian hold the balance of God's sovereignty and grace as well as Calvin. In each sector of the reformation we do however find two or more primary theologians each presenting each element clearly and there is an overall balance. Often it is what are now considered liberal theologians that held the side of grace in place (Barth as an example).

God's sovereignty demands God's justice. A perfect justice has to be perfectly satisfied. We must not focus on the passion of Christ at this point. The suffering in the flesh by Christ is not to be denied or set aside lightly but the focus is on the second death. All men can and according to the Bible will die. Yet no man can satisfy the justice of God because the death mentioned is the

---

[44] HC Q11 - D Head II Art 2 - WCF VIII.5

complete separation from God. Man is separated from God but has the perfect sacrifice as atonement in Christ. This atonement however must be received by faith and that demands life. Yet Christ fully man said from the cross, "[My God, My God why have you forsaken me?" For that moment at least the impossible happens and Christ is feeling not the pain in the flesh but in His soul the pain of being in total darkness separated from God. Then what man cannot do for himself Christ does, Christ returns from the dead speaking both of the flesh and of the spiritual or second death. Why and how can this be? In the flesh Christ knew no sin and His blood was the prefect atoning sacrifice for the sins of others that were laid upon Him. God in the Old Testament had previously declared His flesh would not see corruption. Second is that the sacrifice being acceptable to God, the resurrection was also from prophecy of old. The sect of the Pharisees taught the resurrection and after life of believers before Christ was born. None understood how God was going to do this to include the angels. Christ then made the justice of God as well as God's mercy manifest to men. It is interesting to note that Christ being fully God says no man takes His life but that He lays it down willingly and that He is able to take it up again. This is a reference to the human nature since Christ being God and fully spirit cannot die. We also read Christ was raised by the power of the Holy Spirit and here we read that He was raised by God. Not a contradiction but pointing to the triune nature and perfect unity within the Trinity.

We are dealing with a metaphysical event and terms here that we have trouble with because they defy nature and logic, as we know it. Much like the hypostatic union or perfect union of essential existence of being we discussed earlier. These are not events we can recreate and examine forensically and must be received by faith because God says this is how it is. Thus we indeed see God's justice satisfied and God's mercy revealed, both in Jesus Christ the Son of God.

Questions

1. What did God make manifest when He laid our sins on Christ?

2. What did God pour out on believers in the mercy shown because of the cross?

3. What was Christ raised to on our behalf?

The Belgic Confession of Faith, Article XXI

The Satisfaction of Christ, Our Only High Priest, for Us

We believe that Jesus Christ is ordained with an oath to be an everlasting High Priest, after the order of Melchizedek; and that He has presented Himself in our behalf before the Father, to appease His wrath by His full satisfaction, by offering Himself on the tree of the cross, and pouring out His precious blood to purge away our sins, as the prophets had foretold. For it is written: He was wounded for our transgressions, he was bruised for our iniquities; the chastisement of our peace was upon him; and with his stripes we are healed. He was led as a lamb to the slaughter, and numbered with the transgressors; and condemned by Pontius Pilate as a malefactor, though he had first declared Him innocent. Therefore, He restored that which he took not away, and suffered, the righteous for the unrighteous, as well in His body as in His soul, feeling the terrible punishment which our sins had merited; insomuch that his sweat became as it were great drops of blood falling down upon the ground. He called out: My God, my God, why hast thou forsaken me? and has suffered all this for the remission of our sins.

Wherefore we justly say with the apostle Paul that we know nothing save Jesus Christ, and him crucified; we count all things but loss and refuse for the excellency of the knowledge of Christ Jesus our Lord, in whose wounds we find all manner of consolation. Neither is it necessary to seek or invent any other means of being reconciled to God than this only sacrifice, once offered, by which he hath perfected forever them that are sanctified. This is also the reason why He was called by the angel of God, JESUS, that is to say, SAVIOR, because He would save his people from their sins.[45]

The reference to Christ being ordained with an oath is important to the covenant aspect of Christ as the Mediator. Hebrews 7:20 ff refers to the earthly priests not being ordained with an oath but that Christ was ordained by an oath of God who cannot change or fail. The new covenant is better because of a more sure and infallible Mediator. We find this exact wording in Psalm 110:4.

The choice of the word sanctified in the second paragraph is misfortunate in that it can cause confusion. The proper word at this point would be justified, though it is a truth that the justified are sanctified. However through the ages justification and sanctification have been confused and co-mingled into contortions that are not biblical.

This is an affirmation of saved by faith alone. Though good works will flow of necessity from the regenerated heart, the fact stands that by faith alone man is justified and there is no other condition to be met. It might be well to note here that if a man is justified, the process of sanctification begins immediately and good works will flow from the regenerated by necessity – *by their fruit you shall know them.*

Questions

1. What is the difference between the priesthood of Aaron and Melchizedek?

2. During His passion what did Christ feel and experience in His body?

3. With what words did Christ signify He tasted of the 2nd death for us?

---

[45] HC Q 31 - H XI.16; 17 - WCF VIII.1; 8 - WSC Q23; Q24; Q25; Q26 - WLC Q43; Q44; Q45

The Belgic Confession of Faith, Article XXII
Our Justification Through Faith in Jesus Christ

We believe that, to attain the true knowledge of this great mystery, the Holy Spirit kindles in our hearts an upright faith, which embraces Jesus Christ with all His merits, appropriates Him, and seeks nothing more besides Him. For it must needs follow, either that all things which are requisite to our salvation are not in Jesus Christ, or if all things are in Him, that then those who possess Jesus Christ through faith have complete salvation in Him. Therefore, for any to assert that Christ is not sufficient, but that something more is required besides Him, would be too gross a blasphemy; for hence it would follow that Christ was but half a Savior.

Therefore we justly say with Paul, that we are justified by faith alone, or by faith apart from works. However, to speak more clearly, we do not mean that faith itself justifies us, for it is only an instrument with which we embrace Christ our righteousness. But Jesus Christ, imputing to us all His merits, and so many holy works which He has done for us and in our stead, is our righteousness. And faith is an instrument that keeps us in communion with Him in all His benefits, which, when they become ours, are more than sufficient to acquit us of our sins.[46]

The answer to the so-called Shepherd controversy that is the foundation and fuel for the so-called new theology of Paul contrasted to James is found in the opening statement of this article. Either it is all of Christ or it is none of Christ. This is the biblical and confessional answer. Any who take issue with this must declare themselves out of accord with the standards of the confessions and as an intruder lay the foundation for the exceptions solidly in the infallible Word of God. This has not

---

[46] HC Q20; Q21; Q22; Q23; Q53; Q61 - D Head I.2; 3; 4; 5; 6, Head II.6; 7, Head III & IV 13; 14 - WCF XI.2; XIV.1; 2; 3 - WSC Q85; Q86 - WLC Q72; Q73; Q153

been done as none have stepped up to the plate and declared they are out of accord, but rather the standard writers did not understand. Such arrogance is of the will of man and is outside of both the Bible and the standards of the Reformed church.

The problem arises from a basic error that would say the Bible is not of a unity and can have contradictory statements that require the addition of extra-biblical commentary for the Bible to be understood. God's Word is one and cannot be taken away from or added to. This is the heart of there being a canon and the very essence of the Westminster Confessions' first chapter.

The next error is to try and apply the formulation of divide and then explain the doctrine used by systematic theology to a practical application of theology. For example Shepherd and company place justification and works in parallel and thus add a futuristic element where man is justified and yet continues to justify himself in the good works they insist must accompany justification.

The concept isn't all error in that good works will flow from justification of a necessity (by their fruits you shall know them). This is in accord with the great saved by grace passage of Ephesians two that is the soul of Reformed soteriology. The election must stand or there is no eternal decree and election. Thus, there can be no continuing justification nor chance involved whereby a person by lack of personal action can lose their salvation. The detractors comment concerning works then must be understood in the necessity of the whole of one part flowing form another rather than distinct and parallel events. The five SOLAS of the Reformed church are total confusion if we try to defend each as a complete doctrine. Taken together it can be seen that one will flow from the other of necessity and it doesn't matter with which one a person begins, the other four are present. This is also true with the Reformed TULIP that developed out of the work of the Synod of Dort. Each petal will flow from the others of necessity and mixing the order of presentation will not remove the others from the flower. In soteriology however there is an order for purposes of clarity.

The analogy I prefer at this point with respect to a complete theology is that of the hot air balloon. As we develop one portion of a theology we must use the utmost care not to poke holes in the opposite side of the balloon. As has been said,

"Context, context, context." We must back away and consider the whole of the theology as we develop and tweak individual points.

Another problem develops from decades of theologians that have been trained in systematic theology whereby things are divided into orderly sequences. In practical theology it can be seen that while things flow of necessity one from another, it is also admitted there may not be a measurable division of time as viewed from the perspective of man. Thus it can be said justification and works appear to man to be parallel developments and to try and divide them causes confusion and introduces tension to the biblical texts that do not exist. The early church found the answer to this in dealing with the Trinity and came to the formulation that it is proper for God to eternally exist and for the Son to be eternally begotten of the Father and for the Holy Spirit to eternally proceed from the Father and the Son. The word eternally is key in that eternity is not an infinitely long time line but the complete absence of time as known by the mind of man. Finite minds have a hard time trying to articulate infinite principles. This brings us back to the beginning and all is of Christ or none is of Christ.

We are saved by grace through faith has been the [B]biblical declaration of the Reformed church from her beginning. The same passage continues that God beforehand created good works for the elect to walk in and adds the separation demanded by systematics but does not violate the timing being instantaneous from the perspective of man.

The Bible does not contradict and there is no tension between Paul and James because good works will flow of necessity from justification by faith in Christ alone. Thus Paul can say we are justified by faith and James can point to the necessity of works with faith or else it is a dead faith. This doesn't introduce another kind of faith, for a dead faith is no faith at all.

Questions

1. What does the regeneration of the Holy Spirit bring with it?

2. To believe anything other than Christ is needed for our salvation is what?

3. What is the instrument that keeps believers in communion with Christ?

The Belgic Confession of Faith, Article XXIII

Wherein Our Justification Before God Consists

> We believe that our salvation consists in the remission of our sins for Jesus Christ's sake, and that therein our righteousness before God is implied; as David and Paul teach us, declaring this to be the blessedness of man that God imputes righteousness to him apart from works. And the same apostle says that we are justified freely by his grace, through the redemption that is in Christ Jesus.
>
> And therefore we always hold fast this foundation, ascribing all the glory to God, humbling ourselves before Him, and acknowledging ourselves to be such as we really are, without presuming to trust in anything in ourselves, or in any merit of ours, relying and resting upon the obedience of Christ crucified alone, which becomes ours when we believe in Him. This is sufficient to cover all our iniquities, and to give us confidence in approaching to God; freeing the conscience of fear, terror, and dread, without following the example of our first father, Adam, who, trembling, attempted to cover himself with fig-leaves. And, verily, if we should appear before God, relying on ourselves or on any other creature, though ever so little, we should, alas! be consumed. And therefore every one must pray with David: O Jehovah, enter not into judgment with thy servant: for in thy sight no man living is righteous.[47]

No man living is righteous... A simplistic definition of righteous is the complete obedience to the prevailing law. For the believer the prevailing law is the Word of God, the Bible. We see this in the so-called Great Commission "…. teaching them to

---

[47] HC Q1; Q37; Q38; Q39; Q45; Q56; Q59; Q60 - H XV all - D Head II.3, Rejection 4 - WCF XI all - WSC Q33 - WLC Q69; Q70; Q70

observe all things whatsoever I have commanded." No man ever has or ever will completely obey the law and by the works of the flesh be justified in any way whatsoever before a holy and just God. There is no merit in any work of man before, during or after regeneration. The merit of the completed work of Christ alone is the ground for the righteousness of the believer. That is as stated above the righteousness of Christ is imputed to us, not of our own doing.

Regeneration, adoption, justification, and the continuing work of sanctification flow one from the other of necessity. As Paul notes, "For whom He foreknew, He also predestined [to be] conformed to the image of His Son, that He might be the firstborn among many brethren. Moreover whom He predestined, these He also called; whom He called, these He also justified; and whom He justified, these He also glorified." (Romans 8:29-30)[.] Even the final glorification of the believer is spoken of as past tense because God has spoken and God is able to perform His entire holy will and cannot fail. God names the end from the beginning.

The beginning of sin in the rebellion of Satan against God is found in the desire of the created for autonomy, to be like God. This evil desire of the flesh that Paul names the will of man introduced the heresy of man's ability to either save self or as a minimum be a co-partner with God in man's salvation. From the beginning of the Bible until the end we see this same will of the creature defy the God that created all things. The Bible is clear that all is of Christ or a person is none of Christ's. Yet, the church struggles against the same heresy in every generation to include this present evil day. It is hard for even the elect to understand this evil nature of his will. Paul says it is so prevalent that he finds himself not doing what he should do and in fact doing the thing, which he hates. The total depravity of man is apparent in even the redeemed. The just shall live by faith is declared three times in the Bible. Saving faith is the gift of God and will produce obedience (good works). However the works have nothing to do with justification, but rather are the visible proof of the new man in Christ. The Bible says that if we love Jesus we will obey all of the commands of Jesus. Thus and thus alone could James say that faith without works are dead because true faith will produce works.

Questions

1. Of what does our salvation consist?

2. We rest on what for our salvation?

3. What living man is completely righteous in and of himself?

The Belgic Confession of Faith, Article XXIV

Man's Sanctification and Good Works

We believe that this true faith, being wrought in man by the hearing of the Word of God and the operation of the Holy Spirit, sanctifies him and makes him a new man, causing him to live a new life, and freeing him from the bondage of sin. Therefore it is so far from being true that this justifying faith makes men remiss in a pious and holy life, that on the contrary without it they would never do anything out of love to God, but only out of self-love or fear of damnation. Therefore it is impossible that this holy faith can be unfruitful in man; for we do not speak of a vain faith, but of such a faith which is called in Scripture a faith working through love, which excites man to the practice of those works which God has commanded in His Word.

These works, as they proceed from the good root of faith, are good and acceptable in the sight of God, forasmuch as they are all sanctified by His grace. Nevertheless they are of no account towards our justification, for it is by faith in Christ that we are justified, even before we do good works; otherwise they could not be good works, any more than the fruit of a tree can be good before the tree itself is good.

Therefore we do good works, but not to merit by them (for what can we merit?); nay, we are indebted to God for the good works we do, and not He to us, since it is He who worketh in us both to will and to work, for his good pleasure. Let us therefore attend to what is written: When ye shall have done all the things that are commanded you, say, We are unprofitable servants; we have done that which it was our duty to do. In the meantime we do not deny that God rewards good works, but it is through His grace that He crowns His gifts.

Moreover, though we do good works, we do not found our salvation upon them; for we can do no work but what is polluted by our flesh, and also punishable; and although we could perform such works, still the remembrance of one sin is sufficient to make God reject them. Thus, then, we would always be in doubt, tossed to and fro without any certainty, and our poor consciences would be continually vexed if they relied not on the merits of the suffering and death of our Savior.[48]

Some to show that works are part of true or saving faith have used "Faith working through love," from Ephesians to prove this point. This is an error of the most grievous nature. This confuses sanctification with justification and makes it appear that there is someway a person can fall out of the estate of grace by sin (failure to obey all of God's commands). Man in salvation is freed from the power of sin, not that man in regeneration will no longer sin. Faith produces love toward God and love will produce obedience (works). Is there a time differential between justification, sanctification, and works? Not that we can measure for all are present in regeneration, yet as the Belgic Confession in these last three articles has been so careful to lay before us the truth that works, even in Christ have nothing to do with salvation. Works are visible proof of the inner working of the Holy Spirit as such, though no empirical proof of salvation. Christ says to some at the last day who have been laboring in the name of Christ, depart from me ye that work iniquity, I have never known you. Ephesians 2:8 stands as the only doorway and the foundation of Reformed soteriology. You are saved by grace, through faith, and that not of yourself, it is the gift of God lest any should boast. This leaves no room for such foolish debate as Rome and her false teachers scattered throughout Christendom would lead foolish men to believe.

The error is as old as the heavens and flows from the evil desire of the created to be like God that is to be autonomous.

Questions

---

[48] HC Q32; Q43; Q62; Q63; Q64; Q76; Q86; Q91;Q115; Q122; Q124 - H XVI 2;3;4; 5; 6; 7 - D Head I 13, Head V 13 - WCF XIII 1; 2; 3 - WSC Q35 - WLC Q75; Q77; Q78

1. What sanctifies a person?

2. How many sins does God have to remember to reject all of our so-called good works?

3. What good works are acceptable to God?

The Belgic Confession of Faith, Article XXV

The Abolishing of the Ceremonial Law

We believe that the ceremonies and symbols
of the law ceased at the coming of Christ, and that
all the shadows are accomplished; so that the use
of them must be abolished among Christians; yet
the truth and substance of them remain with us in
Jesus Christ, in whom they have their completion.
In the meantime we still use the testimonies taken
out of the law and the prophets to confirm us in
the doctrine of the gospel, and to regulate our life
in all honorableness to the glory of God,
according to His will.[49]

This is in accordance with the word of Christ when He said
that He had come not to do away with the law but to fulfill it.
Likewise Christ directed that the Jews were to search the
Scriptures for they were that which testified of Him. At the time
of Christ the only Scripture was the Old Testament. Here we find
one of the places this Confession could have used clearer language
to bring the proper understanding to the Reformed tradition
concerning the ceremonial laws. The ceremonial laws did not end
at the birth of Christ, as it might appear the Confession states at
this point. The shadows were lifted in the resurrection and
ascension of Christ, not the moment of His birth or first coming
to earth. To remain sinless as a man Christ had to obey all of the
Old Testament. Without His death there is no testament. In our
day we understand the term last will and testament used to leave
the instructions concerning our estate is of no effect until we die.
This was no different in the day of Christ. As an example we see
Christ tell John the Baptist to baptize Him that they might fulfill
all righteousness. Righteous means complete obedience to the
currently prevailing laws. In life Christ was recognized as a Rabbi
or teacher not a priest much less the high priest. Yet after His
death Christ was made a high priest after the order of Melchizedek
that is without beginning or end. There is a great paradigm shift in
worship because of this priesthood, from the ceremonies of the

[49] HC Q3; Q4; Q92; Q93 - H XII all - D Head III & IV 5 - WCF XIX all - WSC Q39; Q40;
Q41: Q42; Q43; Q44 - WLC Q91; Q92; Q93; Q94; Q95; Q96; Q97; Q98; Q99; Q100; Q101;
Q103; Q104; Q105; Q106

Old Testament to the truth and spirit of the New Testament.

Paul in his letter to the Galatians best explains the necessity of abolishing the old ceremonial laws of the Old Testament (Jews). Paul said this was to enter into bondage again for to be under the law was to maintain perfect obedience to the law. Yet not one person was or will ever be saved by the law. So it was a return not only to the physical obedience of all of the laws of the Old Testament, but to the bondage of sin having made the completed work of Christ of no merit.

Yet the truth and substance of them remain with us is similar to the Westminster Confessions treatment of the judicial laws meant for the nation of Israel as a theocracy. [50] Christ said that man does not live by bread alone but every word that proceeds from the mouth of God. Thus all Scripture is a divine or eternal word and cannot be done away with. To this end Christ also said that not one word or even the smallest mark making up the letters of a word would pass away. Paul in Timothy gives to us a list of the uses of the Scripture and this includes every word of both Testaments. Thus we turn to the New Testament for the complete word or explanation of the Old Testament and the Old Testament for the foundation needed to understand the New Testament. The Bible gives equal weight to all sixty-six books since all are words that proceed from the mouth of God (Present tense intended).

---

[50] Westminster Confession of Faith chapter 19

III. Beside this law, commonly called moral, God was pleased to give to the people of Israel, as a church under age, ceremonial laws, containing several typical ordinances, partly of worship, prefiguring Christ, his graces, actions, sufferings, and benefits;[4] and partly, holding forth divers instructions of moral duties.[5] All which ceremonial laws are now abrogated, under the new testament.[6]

4. Heb. 10:1; Gal. 4:1-3; Col. 2:17; Heb. 9:1-28

5. Lev. 19:9-10, 19, 23, 27; Deut. 24:19-21; see I Cor. 5:7; II Cor. 6:17; Jude 1:23

6. Col. 2:14, 16-17; Dan. 9:27; Eph. 2:15-16; Heb. 9:10; Acts 10:9-16; 11:2-10 IV. To them also, as a body politic, he gave sundry judicial laws, which expired together with the State of that people; not obliging any other now, further than the general equity thereof may require.[7]

7. Exod. 21:1-23:19; Gen. 49:10 with I Peter 2:13-14; I Cor. 9:8-10

Questions

1. What part of the law was fulfilled with the coming of Christ?

2. What part of these abrogated laws remain?

3. What do we use to confirm the Gospel in our lives?

The Belgic Confession of Faith, Article XXVI

Christ's Intercession

We believe that we have no access unto God but alone through the only Mediator and Advocate, Jesus Christ the righteous; who therefore became man, having united in one person the divine and human natures, that we men might have access to the divine Majesty, which access would otherwise be barred against us. But this Mediator, whom the Father has appointed between Him and us, ought in no wise to affright us by His majesty, or cause us to seek another according to our fancy. For there is no creature, either in heaven or on earth, who loves us more than Jesus Christ; who, though existing in the form of God, yet emptied himself, being made in the likeness of men and of a servant for us, and in all things was made like unto his brethren. If, then, we should seek for another mediator who would be favorably inclined towards us, whom could we find who loved us more than He who laid down His life for us, even while we were his enemies? And if we seek for one who has power and majesty, who is there that has so much of both as He who sits at the right hand of God and to whom hath been given all authority in heaven and on earth? And who will sooner be heard than the own well beloved Son of God?

The natural inclination of man to worship demands a God who created all things and rules over his creation. Nature declares this Creator is the God of the Bible. So much so that Paul says in Romans that even those who have never seen or heard the Scriptures know enough to worship the one and only true God. Paul continues that to this natural revelation of God, that God has revealed Himself to natural man, that man knows not only he should worship God alone but understands the Godhead.

Job spoke of the necessity of a days-man (spokesman or mediator) being necessary between God and man. Out of doubt and fear alone man will seek a god. The Confession at this point gives both logical and philosophical reasons why this Mediator must be Christ. When the Confession says here we have no access except through Christ it is speaking of our position in grace with God by the completed work of Christ. This does not mean it is not possible for us to speak to God the Father such as when we pray in the Lord's Prayer addressing God the Father.

> Therefore it was only through distrust that this practice of dishonoring, instead of honoring, the saints was introduced, doing that which they never have done nor required, but have on the contrary steadfastly rejected according to their bounden duty, as appears by their writings. Neither must we plead here our unworthiness; for the meaning is not that we should offer our prayers to God on the ground of our own worthiness, but only on the ground of the excellency and worthiness of the Lord Jesus Christ, whose righteousness is become ours by faith.

The long-standing battle between the Church of Rome and the Johnny-come-lately of the 17th century concerning justification by faith alone should be put to rest with this one short statement. It wasn't and continues today. Man from the beginning has demanded autonomy but was not the originator of this rebellion against the sovereignty of God. It began with the fall of Satan who desired to be like God and to ascend on high of his own power. Satan later tempts the first of God's children in the garden with this same lie, "you can be like God." Whereas the Church of Rome honors and worships the saints of the church having risen to such status by the declarations of man, these same saints (as all believers are) would never have done the same thing in their own day. The Bible explicitly forbids worship of any but God.

> Therefore the apostle, to remove this foolish fear, or rather distrust, from us, rightly says that Jesus Christ in all things was made like unto his brethren, that he might become a merciful and faithful high priest, to make propitiation for the sins of the people. For in that he himself hath suffered being tempted, he is able to succor them that are tempted. And further to encourage us to

go to Him, he says: Having then a great high priest, who hath passed through the heavens, Jesus the Son of God, let us hold fast our confession. For we have not a high priest that cannot be touched with the feeling of our infirmities; but one that hath been in all points tempted like as we are, yet without sin. Let us therefore draw near with boldness unto the throne of grace, that we may receive mercy, and may find grace to help us in time of need. The same apostle says: Having boldness to enter into the holy place by the blood of Jesus, let us draw near with a true heart in fullness of faith, etc. Likewise: Christ hath his priesthood unchangeable; wherefore also he is able to save to the uttermost them that draw near unto God through him, seeing he ever liveth to make intercession for them.

While the shedding of blood was a necessity for the atonement (Without the shedding of blood there is no remission of sin) and this would have made the incarnation and the assumption of human form a necessity the real comfort from the humanity of Christ comes from Christ having been where we are and thus enabled to fully understand our need for a mediator. Note that the Confession continually refers to the errors of worship outside the blood of Christ as mistrust. This means that in denial of the clear teaching of Scripture man does not fully trust God for all things, but attempts to add his own efforts to those of God because man mistrusts the ability of God to accomplish His entire holy will.

What more can be required? since Christ Himself says: I am the way, and the truth, and the life: no one cometh unto the Father, but by me. To what purpose should we, then, seek another advocate, since it has pleased God to give us His own Son as an Advocate? Let us not forsake Him to take another, or rather to seek after another, without ever being able to find him; for God well knew, when He gave Him to us, that we were sinners.

An appeal to logic as such once more employed by the

confession to show the foolishness of attempting to cover sins with anything other than the blood of Christ. Any but the most profound fool can see from the Word of God that there is no other Mediator and to seek such is pure foolishness and that another will not be found for none exists. When God said there should be no other gods before me, God was not saying there are other Gods and the Bible clearly teaches that all other gods are the mere foolishness of the imagination of man. Yet, this has not stopped the created, angels and men, from attempting to enter into will worship and to be like God.

> Therefore, according to the command of Christ, we call upon the heavenly Father through Jesus Christ our only Mediator, as we are taught in the Lord's Prayer; being assured that whatever we ask of the Father in His Name will be granted us.

I would hastily add to this paragraph that whatever we ask is conditional in that all such requests to be valid must be in the will of God. The litmus test for such a request then must be obtained to returning to the purpose for which God created all things, God's own glory. The question does it glorify God must be asked and the Scriptures diligently searched with prayer then, less in our boldness we inadvertently sin against God with frivolous prayers born of the lust of the flesh and not the indwelling Holy Spirit.

Questions

1. What does the confession mean when it says we have no access to God except through Jesus Christ?

2. What does this have to do with Christ being our High Priest?

3. Where does our boldness to approach God come from?

The Belgic Confession of Faith, Article XXVII

The Catholic Christian Church

We believe and profess one catholic or universal Church, which is a holy congregation of true Christian believers, all expecting their salvation in Jesus Christ, being washed by His blood, sanctified and sealed by the Holy Spirit.

This Church has been from the beginning of the world, and will be to the end thereof; which is evident from this that Christ is an eternal King, which without subjects He cannot be. And this holy Church is preserved or supported by God against the rage of the whole world; though it sometimes for a while appears very small, and in the eyes of men to be reduced to nothing; as during the perilous reign of Ahab the Lord reserved unto Him seven thousand men who had not bowed their knees to Baal.

Furthermore, this holy Church is not confined, bound, or limited to a certain place or to certain persons, but is spread and dispersed over the whole world; and yet is joined and united with heart and will, by the power of faith, in one and the same Spirit[51].

Two important things are found in this very short article:

1. The church has existed from the moment of creation. Christ did not come into existence in the incarnation, but has eternally existed as a co-equal to God. As noted here Christ has always been the King and being a king requires subjects. How foolish then of those that refer to themselves as New Testament churches as if this in some way relieves them from the burden of the law of the Old Testament.

2. The proliferation of denominations and more especially

---

[51] HC Q54 - H XVII all - WCF XXV all - WLC Q61; Q62; Q63; Q64

the wild growth the world is experiencing in non-church groups scattered to the four winds in what some have labeled the post-denominational age is the biggest denial of the Holy Spirit all claim to be led by that can exist among men.

The Holy Spirit seals believers. The Holy Spirit will forever lead mankind to all truth and bring unity, never division to the body of Christ. Nonetheless, throughout history we find men who cannot find a place of rest within an existing church and begin new denominations or of a much more non-biblical nature, independent churches or groups gathering in various homes. They claim that they are following the Holy Spirit and are the ones worshipping God, as God would have it be. To which I say why did the 7000 in the day of Ahab not begin another group of chosen people? Why did they not separate themselves and worship outside the temple as God had commanded? Dare any suggest that this holy remnant preserved by God had not the wisdom or courage to follow where the Holy Spirit led. Where the Spirit led them was to refrain from the temptations and stains of the world and those evil ones within the chosen people and to worship God only as God had commanded.

One Lord, one Spirit, one body, one baptism stands firm in the onslaught of mankind to create his own system of worship after his own imagination in denial of the revealed truth of God and rebellion against God. Paul said where division exists man is yet carnal and in need of the milk of the Gospel. Babies should not be planting so-called new churches. The true church of God transcends all of these divisions and man made boundaries and worships God in truth and spirit. God is spirit and God requires such to worship Him alone.

To worship in truth means to worship God only as God has commanded in the Bible. The Bible is the only truth in existence on earth. To worship God in Spirit means from the inner most being, naturally as a child worships his parents, not of man's knowledge, but the knowledge of God given to all of His creation. God's Word is food for the soul.

Questions

1. What does it mean to worship God in truth?

2. What does it mean to worship God in spirit?

3. What must regulate how we worship God?

The Belgic Confession of Faith, Article XXVIII
Every One Is Bound to Join Himself to the True Church

We believe, since this holy congregation is an assembly of those who are saved, and outside of it there is no salvation, that no person of whatsoever state or condition he may be, ought to withdraw from it, content to be by himself; but that all men are in duty bound to join and unite themselves with it; maintaining the unity of the Church; submitting themselves to the doctrine and discipline thereof; bowing their necks under the yoke of Jesus Christ; and as mutual members of the same body, serving to the edification of the brethren, according to the talents God has given them.

And that this may be the more effectually observed, it is the duty of all believers, according to the Word of God, to separate themselves from all those who do not belong to the Church, and to join themselves to this congregation, where so ever God has established it, even though the magistrates and edicts of princes were against it, yea, though they should suffer death or any other corporal punishment. Therefore all those who separate themselves from the same or do not join themselves to it act contrary to the ordinance of God.[52]

Matthew 16:18 says that Christ builds the church. To deny the necessity of the church is tantamount to saying that Jesus Christ made an error in founding the church. The foundation of Christian discipline found in Matthew 18 is pure vanity apart from the necessity of the church. This was a problem in the reformation of the sixteenth century but no new comer to the church scene as such. We find in Hebrews 10:25 that there were those even at this early date who did not honor the sacred assembly of the church and thus did not attend these assemblies.

---

[52] H XVII all - WCF XXV all

The so called house church movement of today holds the "institutionalized" or formal church in total disdain and declares it no church.[53] They have no professional clergy and abhor paid staff. Not to be, for outside the church there is no salvation. This doesn't limit God as it might first appear, but appeals to the covenant nature of God and that the body of Christ is one body even as Father, Son, and Holy Spirit are one God. Thus the understanding that in regeneration a true believer will find his place in the church of Christ.

While the proliferation of denominations and churches today seems to be unbiblical and many divisions seem to be over things indifferent, it stands that [God has allowed this diversity of churches to come into existence and in most God's love and grace can be seen as proof of God's presence. Into this diversity of churches there is no reason for any believer to remain outside the body and to attempt to walk and worship alone.

Christ founded the church, the Holy Spirit made it manifest at Pentecost, and God has preserved the church through the centuries by the power of His Word alone, that all might be partakers of the same body and indwelled by the same Spirit and enabled to accomplish all of God's holy will despite all opposition of the devil in this temporal world.

Questions

1. Who founded the church?

2. When was the church made manifest as a human institution or visible on earth? (Not considering the ancient Jewish church as being the church in the wilderness)

3. That the church might uniformly be more visible what is the duty of all believers?

---

[53] This is a reference to parts of the emergent/.emerging church and others and in no way condemns the assembly of lawful bodies of Christ meeting wherever they can.

The Belgic Confession of Faith, Article XXIX

The Marks of the True Church, and Wherein it Differs from the False Church

We believe that we ought diligently and circumspectly to discern from the Word of God which is the true Church, since all sects which are in the world assume to themselves the name of the Church. But we speak not here of hypocrites, who are mixed in the Church with the good, yet are not of the Church, though externally in it; but we say that the body and communion of the true Church must be distinguished from all sects that call themselves the Church.

The marks by which the true Church is known are these: If the pure doctrine of the gospel is preached therein; if it maintains the pure administration of the sacraments as instituted by Christ; if church discipline is exercised in chastening [1] of sin; in short, if all things are managed according to the pure Word of God, all things contrary thereto rejected, and Jesus Christ acknowledged as the only Head of the Church. Hereby the true Church may certainly be known, from which no man has a right to separate himself.

With respect to those who are members of the Church, they may be known by the marks of Christians; namely, by faith, and when, having received Jesus Christ the only Savior, they avoid sin, follow after righteousness, love the true God and their neighbor, neither turn aside to the right or left, and crucify the flesh with the works thereof. But this is not to be understood as if there did not remain in them great infirmities; but they fight against them through the Spirit all the days of their life, continually taking their refuge in the blood, death, passion, and obedience of our Lord

Jesus Christ, in whom they have remission of sins, through faith in Him.

As for the false Church, it ascribes more power and authority to itself and its ordinances than to the Word of God, and will not submit itself to the yoke of Christ. Neither does it administer the sacraments as appointed by Christ in His Word, but adds to and takes from them, as it thinks proper; it relies more upon men than upon Christ; and persecutes those who live holy according to the Word of God and rebuke it for its errors, covetousness, and idolatry.

These two Churches are easily known and distinguished from each other.

1.   "Punishing" has been changed to "chastening". [54]

Well written and these are the three classic marks of the true church. That these churches are easily known seems at first glance to be an overstatement. However it is written, *by their fruits you shall know them*. In the classic definition of salvation by faith alone (Eph. 2:8) we see Paul continue to point out that the believer will walk in the good works that God created for them to walk in before the foundation of the world. James words it a bit differently but to the same end when he says that he will show you his faith by his works.

One of the key points to examine then is what are good works. Good works are not what is good from the perception of man but that which bring glory to God. Thus two people doing the same thing, one for any motivation except the glory of God and the other in Christ for the glory of God alone defines good works. Therefore good work is not in the deed, but in the heart of the performer of the work and the motivation thereunto.

The last mark is Christian discipline, which is never as punishment or the extracting of the proverbial pound of flesh for deed done, but of restoration of a brother to the fellowship of Christ (Mt. 18).

---

[54] H XVII 8; 9; 10; 11; 12; 13; 14; 15

Questions

1. What are the marks of the true church?

2. Other than these marks how do we measure a church or believer?

3. Why is church discipline a necessity and a mark of the true church?

The Belgic Confession of Faith, Article XXX

The Government of the Church and its Offices

We believe that this true Church must be governed by that spiritual polity which our Lord has taught us in His Word; namely, that there must be ministers or pastors to preach the Word of God and to administer the sacraments; also elders and deacons, who, together with the pastors, form the council of the Church; that by these means the true religion may be preserved, and the true doctrine everywhere propagated, likewise transgressors chastened [1] and restrained by spiritual means; also that the poor and distressed may be relieved and comforted, according to their necessities. By these means everything will be carried on in the Church with good order and decency, when faithful men are chosen, according to the rule prescribed by St. Paul in his Epistle to Timothy.

1. "Punished" has been changed to "chastened".[55]

All Reformed churches will agree that we are to be ruled by the form of government given to us in the Bible. The form here is the same throughout the history of the continental Reformed churches, and except for some minor variations isn't that different than the Presbyterian churches of Scotland and England. Many refer to a difference of perspective from the two sides of the English Channel and the government of the churches. This is a false dichotomy in that none will deny this foundational statement and it is in the refinement of polity in churches ruled by elders we see a parliamentary difference, not of beliefs.

For example the "Reformed" have consistories and the Presbyterians sessions. Likewise the higher courts are Classis and Presbytery though there is a difference at this point as to where the membership of the pastors (clergy) lies. The Reformed hold the pastor accountable to a local church and the Presbyterians

---

[55] HC Q82; Q83; Q84; Q85 - H XIV 5;6 - WCF I.6 XXX.1; 2;3; 4

have clergy as a member of this so-called higher court without membership in a local church. This means in Presbyterian churches the pastor is still accountable to the session as such but all matters of discipline or question is handled by Presbytery where the pastor's membership is held.

Both systems have in common that the real power of order lies with the local church, though in practice we often find this is corrupted. The question of jurisdiction also arises and is handled somewhat differently. This is of minor concern in that the underlying reliance on the Bible, the necessity of the church, and how the Word and sacraments are handled is the crucial issue since these are marks of being a part of the true body of Christ, not the polity of the particular church. Of more importance is that both systems deny any head of the church other than Jesus Christ and do not create offices that place one elder above another in a supposed order of hierarchy.

Proper execution of the propagation of the Gospel and the discipline of the church cannot be obtained in other systems. The current slide into sin and liberalism of the majority of Episcopalian systems of government testify to the truth revealed here from the 16th century reformers. This doesn't condemn other systems of church government, just states that that listed is the most biblical and the way to avoid the error of man as much as can be in the flesh. All systems will give lip service to some of this, but nothing short of continental Reformed holds it in this exact format. The appeal to Paul is valid and that in reality can be reduced to one short phrase, "all things decently and in order." Order in the churches is essential! The Bible is silent on much of the fine detail and therefore it should not be a divisive issue in our churches.

Questions

1. What advantage does the [C]church ruled by elders have over other forms of church government?

2. What is the scriptural way of governing the [C]church?

3. What does church government have to do with the poor and distressed?

The Belgic Confession of Faith, Article XXXI

The Ministers, Elders, and Deacons

We believe that the ministers of God's Word, the elders, and the deacons ought to be chosen to their respective offices by a lawful election by the Church, with calling upon the name of the Lord, and in that order which the Word of God teaches. Therefore every one must take heed not to intrude himself by improper means, but is bound to wait till it shall please God to call him; that he may have testimony of his calling, and be certain and assured that it is of the Lord.

As for the ministers of God's Word, they have equally the same power and authority wheresoever they are, as they are all ministers of Christ, the only universal Bishop and the only Head of the Church.

Moreover, in order that this holy ordinance of God may not be violated or slighted, we say that every one ought to esteem the ministers of God's Word and the elders of the Church very highly for their work's sake, and be at peace with them without murmuring, strife, or contention, as much as possible.[56]

The Reformed have always looked to a threefold calling to office in the church. 1. The sense of calling by God to a particular office in the church by the individual. 2. The acknowledgement of that call by the congregation to which the person belongs. 3. The official call, ordination, and installation of the person to the work of the particular office by a recognized court of the church. All offices in the church are ordained offices. The modern practice of professional lay people who earn their keep so to speak within the church courts was a foreign thought to the reformers.

There is no difference between elders in the church. Most hold a three office position here as Pastor, elder, deacon. Many have blended the call of eldership and only have two offices,

---

[56] HC Q84; Q85 - H XVIII all - WCF XXX - XXXI

whereas they distinguish between those called as pastors and those called as elders in the church by title and duty only. There should be three distinct offices per the Bible and this confusion of offices in the church is part of the disrespect we see for the office of minister as a whole today, and is an affront to God who specifically listed the officers given to the church from God as opposed to those called of God to serve in a particular church alone (elders and deacons). Pastors properly called and ordained belong to the whole church. They should be respected for the office and God's calling more than their own actions. There are mechanisms in place for men who fail their call or who have sneaked in by ungodly methods or for ungodly motivations. Among men this will be part of the ministerial scene and places no stigma on the office which the Bible demands all respect and to listen to these God ordained officers in ordering the worship and activities of the church.

So while there is no hierarchy within the eldership per se', there is a place of office in order of things that should be maintained and respected. This isn't unlike the Godhead where none can biblically debate the equality, yet all would also be unable to produce biblical grounds there is not a distinction of office within the Godhead. This is a key concept to understand. We also see this understanding as key for the place of man and woman within the church and of husband and wife in marriage. Until we understand this three-office issue, we will not understand the full implication of the Fifth Commandment or how all our earthly relationships should reflect the relationship that exists within the Godhead.

Questions

1. How are officers chosen in the local [C]church?

2. Who is the only bishop in Reformed churches?

3. Why should everyone esteem ministers of the Gospel?

The Belgic Confession of Faith, Article XXXII

The Order and Discipline of the Church

>In the meantime we believe, though it is useful and beneficial that those who are rulers of the Church institute and establish certain ordinances among themselves for maintaining the body of the Church, yet that they ought studiously to take care that they do not depart from those things which Christ, our only Master, has instituted. And therefore we reject all human inventions, and all laws which man would introduce into the worship of God, thereby to bind and compel the conscience in any manner whatever. Therefore we admit only of that which tends to nourish and preserve concord and unity, and to keep all men in obedience to God. For this purpose, excommunication or church discipline is requisite, with all that pertains to it, according to the Word of God.[57]

Discipline is the third mark of the true church. It may be the most neglected and misunderstood doctrine of the church. Worship is only as God commanded and the officers of the church are commanded to maintain the peace, unity, and order of the church. This order cannot be obtained without rules or orders within the church which of necessity come from the pens of man. These rules of man cannot bind the conscience of any, only God's revealed Word may do that. Nonetheless the authority to make rules is passed to the church by the word of Christ who said to you I give the power to bind and loose. Binding and losing is a legal term and has to do with what rules are binding upon the people. In other words Christ gave to the church this specific authority to make the rules of worship and order in the church.

If and only if all of the churches would continue in the fellowship of Christ and recognize each other can or will proper Christian discipline be effective. By nature the rebellion that lives

---

[57] HC Q84 - H XVIII all

within the flesh and ego of man will not bow to rules, even God's Word willingly. Among men there will be strife from time to time and the issue of sin must be dealt with constantly. If the relationship of the church to the individual member is of no value to that person they will not hear admonishment and move to another church and begin again sowing division and strife wherever they go. Because the churches do not recognize the authority of each other the new church welcomes the unrepentant sinner and adds evil to the holiness that existed prior to the arrival of this fugitive from God's discipline.

The church that consistently practices Christian discipline is not the largest church in the community. Here then is the rub so to speak, the friction between the order of discipline and the rolls of the church. The church will not have peace, unity, and prosperity apart from discipline but in blindness the church sees discipline as that which stunts church growth and mission. The real issue here is that without discipline there is no unity of spirit nor will God bless the church. Peace with God comes from obedience to God.

All discipline is intended to reclaim that which is lost and the restoration of a sinner to the family of God. Even excommunication is to work repentance and reconciliation. This does not happen when the church on the other corner doesn't recognize the discipline of her next-door sister church. Even within Reformed churches the cross-denominational aspect of church discipline fails miserably to the detriment of the church of God on earth.

Questions

1. What is the purpose of church discipline?

2. What are the officers of the church commanded by God to do?

3. Is excommunication a valid form of church discipline?

The Belgic Confession of Faith, Article XXXIII

The Sacraments

We believe that our gracious God, taking account of our weakness and infirmities, has ordained the sacraments for us, thereby to seal unto us His promises, and to be pledges of the good will and grace of God towards us, and also to nourish and strengthen our faith; which He has joined to the Word of the gospel, the better to present to our senses both that which He declares to us by His Word and that which He works inwardly in our hearts, thereby confirming in us the salvation which He imparts to us. For they are visible signs and seals of an inward and invisible thing, by means whereof God works in us by the power of the Holy Spirit. Therefore the signs are not empty or meaningless, so as to deceive us. For Jesus Christ is the true object presented by them, without whom they would be of no moment.

Moreover, we are satisfied with the number of sacraments which Christ our Lord has instituted, which are two only, namely, the sacrament of baptism and the holy supper of our Lord Jesus Christ.[58]

This chapter assigns the definition as such of the Reformed churches throughout history to the sacraments as signs and seals of entrance into the covenant of grace. The sacraments do two things in that at once they give to man a visible element of the covenant to which they point. The sacraments have their context within the covenant of grace alone.

Man needs this visible, physical element of religion or faith. The chosen people demanded a golden calf even as the mountain thundered above them from the voice of God. While this was an idol and understood by the created from the beginning as sin though the law had not been given to reveal this sin yet, the

---

[58] HC Q65; Q66; Q67; Q68 - H XIII 3; 4; 5 XIX all - D Head III & IV Art 17; Head V 14 - WCF XXVII all - WSC Q85; Q88; Q89; Q90; Q91; Q92; Q93 - WLC Q153 thru Q159

people were not attempting to create another God as much as trying to make the God they feared and were listening to the thunder of visible in their midst. While this people had the sign of circumcision and the promise, they needed more and sinned in their attempt to meet this need of physical worship as well as spiritual.

Man is not that different today or was he in the reformation. This statement then is of necessity less the church adds to the ordinances of God. Thus the clear claim of only two signs or sacraments. God alone commands how He is to be worshiped and represented to the world. God chose Word and sacrament as His representation in the world. To that man may add nothing.

Questions

1. What are the two sacraments of the Christian Church?

2. Where does the marriage ceremony or burial ceremony enter into this?

3. What are the sacraments?

The Belgic Confession of Faith, Article XXXIV

Holy Baptism

We believe and confess that Jesus Christ, who is the end of the law, has made an end, by the shedding of His blood, of all other sheddings of blood which men could or would make as a propitiation or satisfaction for sin; and that He, having abolished circumcision, which was done with blood, has instituted the sacrament of baptism instead thereof; by which we are received into the Church of God, and separated from all other people and strange religions, that we may wholly belong to Him whose mark and ensign we bear; and which serves as a testimony to us that He will forever be our gracious God and Father.

The exchange of a bloody sacrament unto death for a spiritual sacrament unto life is a fulfillment of the shadow of the former for the reality of the present. The fulfillment is not abolishment of the need of the sacrament that marks God's people on earth and binds them to God in the covenant. That which pointed to the coming Messiah fulfilled by Christ, once and for all time. The type replaced by the light of the anti-type. Thus Christ said search the Scriptures for they are that which speak of me.

Therefore He has commanded all those who are His to be baptized with pure water, into the name of the Father and of the Son and of the Holy Spirit, thereby signifying to us, that as water washes away the filth of the body when poured upon it, and is seen on the body of the baptized when sprinkled upon him, so does the blood of Christ by the power of the Holy Spirit internally sprinkle the soul, cleanse it from its sins, and regenerate us from children of wrath unto children of God. Not that this is effected by the external water, but by the sprinkling of the precious blood of the Son of God; who is our Red Sea, through which we must pass to escape the tyranny of Pharaoh, that is, the devil, and to enter into the spiritual land of Canaan.[59]

Read this whole paragraph as one part or you will fall into the error of baptismal regeneration. Regeneration is not tied to baptism in anyway whatsoever. It is a truth that the regenerate will be baptized, but not of necessity as if regeneration depended on the sign. The type was seen in the crossing of the Red sea by the infant nation of Israel with Moses, whereby all were under or sprinkled by the water. Peter speaks of this very type and that baptism is the antitype in almost the same words used in this paragraph.

> The ministers, therefore, on their part administer the sacrament and that which is visible, but our Lord gives that which is signified by the sacrament, namely, the gifts and invisible grace; washing, cleansing, and purging our souls of all filth and unrighteousness; renewing our hearts and filling them with all comfort; giving unto us a true assurance of His fatherly goodness; putting on us the new man, and putting off the old man with all his deeds.

For the elect and thereby regenerate the baptism will be completely effective. As the water marks the outside of the regenerate, so the Holy Spirit replaces the heart of stone with a heart of flesh and turns the sinner toward God in sanctification. Use care these things are not the inner act of God in the Holy Spirit, but point to them. In other words all these things are present and baptism is after the fact so to speak in obedience to God's Word. In type He commanded all male Jews to be circumcised, in anti-type He commands all believers to be baptized as a sign of the inner seal of the Holy Spirit accomplishing these things.

> We believe, therefore, that every man who is earnestly studious of obtaining life eternal ought to be baptized but once with this only baptism, without ever repeating the same, since we cannot be born twice. Neither does this baptism avail us only at the time when the water is poured upon us

[59] HC Q69 thru Q74 - H XX all - WCF XXVIII all - WSC Q94; Q95 - WLC Q165; Q166; Q167

and received by us, but also through the whole course of our life.

This should be a clear analogy, as you can only be naturally born once, so you can only be spiritually born once. That spiritual birth being marked by baptism is not in time, thus baptism by the church in proper form, that is the name of the Father, Son, and Holy Spirit is efficacious in God's time and needs not be repeated. Indeed, repetition would defame the name of Christ as if Christ could be offered on the altar again.

> Therefore we detest the error of the Anabaptists, who are not content with the one only baptism they have once received, and moreover condemn the baptism of the infants of believers, who we believe ought to be baptized and sealed with the sign of the covenant, as the children in Israel formerly were circumcised upon the same promises which are made unto our children. And indeed Christ shed His blood no less for the washing of the children of believers than for adult persons; and therefore they ought to receive the sign and sacrament of that which Christ has done for them; as the Lord commanded in the law that they should be made partakers of the sacrament of Christ's suffering and death shortly after they were born, by offering for them a lamb, which was a sacrament of Jesus Christ. Moreover, what circumcision was to the Jews, baptism is to our children. And for this reason St. Paul calls baptism the circumcision of Christ.

Questions

1. What must be present with the external application of the minister to make the sacrament effective?

2. What reasoning does the confession use to point out the truth of only one baptism for life?

3. What two errors of the Anabaptists does the Confession in this article particularly detest?

The Belgic Confession of Faith, Article XXXV

The Holy Supper of Our Lord Jesus Christ

We believe and confess that our Savior Jesus Christ did ordain and institute the sacrament of the holy supper to nourish and support those whom He has already regenerated and incorporated into His family, which is His Church.

There is real communion (communication) with Christ in the Lord's Supper and this can only be true for the believer. Those who are not of the family will bring condemnation upon themselves and not blessing. That is they will not receive of grace but condemnation in improperly coming to the table. (See the parable of the wedding feast)

Now those who are regenerated have in them a twofold life, the one corporal and temporal, which they have from the first birth and is common to all men; the other, spiritual and heavenly, which is given them in their second birth, which is effected by the Word of the gospel, in the communion of the body of Christ; and this life is not common, but is peculiar to God's elect. In like manner God has given us, for the support of the bodily and earthly life, earthly and common bread, which is subservient thereto and is common to all men, even as life itself. But for the support of the spiritual and heavenly life which believers have He has sent a living bread, which descended from heaven, namely, Jesus Christ, who nourishes and strengthens the spiritual life of believers when they eat Him, that is to say, when they appropriate and receive Him by faith in the spirit.[60]

Thus the sacraments are also called means of grace in that there is a real partaking of Christ in the Supper. Not the actual feeding upon Christ as if meat, but feeding of the spirit born of Christ.

[60] HC Q75 thru Q80- WCF XXIX all - WSC Q96; Q97 - WLC Q168 thru Q175

In order that He might represent unto us this spiritual and heavenly bread, Christ has instituted an earthly and visible bread as a sacrament of His body, and wine as a sacrament of His blood, to testify by them unto us that, as certainly as we receive and hold this sacrament in our hands and eat and drink the same with our mouths, by which our life is afterwards nourished, we also do as certainly receive by faith (which is the hand and mouth of our soul) the true body and blood of Christ our only Savior in our souls, for the support of our spiritual life.

In contrast to those who see the bread and wine transformed into the actual flesh and blood of Christ, the Reformed have always maintained the reality of the Table without the monstrous thought believers are cannibals eating the flesh of Christ. The argument for actual change of substance and the spiritual understanding of the Table is much older than the reformation. There were great debates in the ninth century concerning this very thing. The reformers here as in many places choose the biblical doctrine that has been in the church from her founding in Jerusalem on the day of Pentecost. The reformation was not all new doctrine but the discernment of biblical doctrine that had been buried beneath Roman Catholic tradition and dogma to the detriment of the body of Christ and harm of God's people in withholding the means of grace from the people.

Now, as it is certain and beyond all doubt that Jesus Christ has not enjoined to us the use of His sacraments in vain, so He works in us all that He represents to us by these holy signs, though the manner surpasses our understanding and cannot be comprehended by us, as the operations of the Holy Spirit are hidden and incomprehensible. In the meantime we err not when we say that what is eaten and drunk by us is the proper and natural body and the proper blood of Christ. But the manner of our partaking of the same is not by the mouth, but by the spirit through faith. Thus, then, though Christ always sits at the right hand of His Father in the heavens, yet does He not therefore cease to make us partakers of Himself by faith. This feast is a spiritual table, at which Christ communicates Himself with all His benefits to us, and gives us there to enjoy both Himself and the merits of His sufferings and death: nourishing, strengthening, and comforting our poor comfortless souls by the eating of His flesh, quickening and refreshing them by the drinking of His blood.

Since the doctrine of the Roman Church from which the Reformed churches were born has been in deep heresy for several centuries we find the need of clarity and redundancy in dealing with this issue. It is in reality the body and blood of Christ, but not physically but spiritually discerned.

Further, though the sacraments are connected with the thing signified nevertheless both are not received by all men. The ungodly indeed receives the sacrament to his condemnation, but he does not receive the truth of the sacrament, even as Judas and Simon the sorcerer both indeed received the sacrament but not Christ who was signified by it, of whom believers only are made partakers.

Christ is in the sacrament, the sacrament is real, but not so joined that physical partaking of the sacrament is the spiritual receipt of the sacrament or the thing signified, union with Christ. Christ, the Word of God cannot thus be separated from the sacrament, but neither may the unbeliever in the sacrament wrongly receive Him.

Lastly, we receive this holy sacrament in the assembly of the people of God, with humility and reverence, keeping up among us a holy remembrance of the death of Christ our Savior, with thanksgiving, making there confession of our faith and of the Christian religion. Therefore no one ought to come to this table without having previously rightly examined himself, lest by eating of this bread and drinking of this cup he eat and drink judgment to himself. In a word, we are

moved by the use of this holy sacrament to a
fervent love towards God and our neighbor.

The table in that it is the body and blood of Christ and is real
communion with Christ is holy and to approach this table without
confession and prayer in self-examination is failure to discern the
body and blood of Christ. While it is true this is the place for
those troubled and in doubt that they might make use of this
means of grace, it is to be approached most seriously and
reverently. For this reason among others, the sacrament then is
only rightly presented in connection with the Word in the sacred
assembly of the church.

Therefore we reject all mixtures and
damnable inventions which men have added unto
and blended with the sacraments, as profanations
of them; and affirm that we ought to rest satisfied
with the ordinance which Christ and His apostles
have taught us, and that we must speak of them in
the same manner as they have spoken.

Being part of the Word, the sacrament is to be handled the
same way, with reverence and prayer. Like the Scriptures it is not
to be diminished nor added to in any way whatsoever. Connected,
as it is to the worship of God's people of Him alone, it is rightly
also within the veil of the Regulated Principle of Worship.

Questions

1.   To not properly prepare and partake of the table is a
     failure to do what?

2.   How are we to receive the elements of the sacrament?

3.   What do we receive from Christ at His Table?

4. **The Belgic Confession of Faith, Article XXXVI**

The Magistracy (Civil Government)

> We believe that our gracious God, because of
> the depravity of mankind, has appointed kings,
> princes, and magistrates; willing that the world
> should be governed by certain laws and policies;
> to the end that the dissoluteness of men might be
> restrained, and all things carried on among them
> with good order and decency. For this purpose He
> has invested the magistracy with the sword for the
> punishment of evil-doers and for the protection of
> them that do well.[61]

God instituted civil government. Many see this in shadow in the flood narrative of Genesis where God declares that he who sheds blood will have his blood spilled by men, the institution as such of capital punishment.

> Their office is not only to have regard unto
> and watch for the welfare of the civil state, but
> also to protect the sacred ministry, that the
> kingdom of Christ may thus be promoted. They
> must therefore countenance the preaching of the
> Word of the gospel everywhere, that God may be
> honored and worshipped by every one, as He
> commands in His Word.

The ancient church corrupted this and as early as 300 AD we see the church and state become one and seek power over others. While God's word places them beside each other and specifically gives to the civil government the sword, neither was for the purpose of creating personal kingdoms on earth, but for the propagation and protection of the church. The two cannot be combined without the result being an admixture from hell itself.

> Moreover, it is the bounden duty of every
> one, of whatever state, quality, or condition he
> may be, to subject himself to the magistrates; to
> pay tribute, to show due honor and respect to

---

[61] HC Q101; Q104; Q105 - H XXX all - WCF XXIII all

> them, and to obey them in all things which are not
> repugnant to the Word of God; to supplicate for
> them in their prayers that God may rule and guide
> them in all their ways, and that we may lead a
> tranquil and quiet life in all godliness and gravity.

The [church from the beginning has missed this mark of the Church established in the Bible. This Confession here adds the idea of disobedience where the civil government is doing things sinful (repugnant to God). This is not Scriptural! There is no word from Christ that suggests disobedience because the government is evil. Christ uttered not one word against the government of His day that imprisoned and then beheaded John the Baptist, the greatest prophet to have graced the flesh of man. Rather Christ commanded the people render unto Caesar the things of Caesar. This is also contrary to Romans 13.

> Wherefore we detest the Anabaptists and
> other seditious people, and in general all those
> who reject the higher powers and magistrates and
> would subvert justice, introduce community of
> goods, and confound that decency and good order
> which God has established among men.

The church began as a communist commune. This offends some, but the fact is they had all things in common. However the evil within the flesh brought forth the greed and sluggishness of some from the start. So much so that Paul said in one place those whom did not work would not eat. Very early we see the Gentiles complaining they were not getting a proper distribution of these common goods. Communism promotes corruption and was dropped as the means of existence for one of sacrificial giving in stewardship very early in the New Testament. The Anabaptists would have continued this cancer among the people of the reformation.

Questions

1. Why does the Confession say God appointed kings and magistrates to accomplish?

2. Besides obedience what should a believer be doing for magistrates?

3. What error of the Anabaptists is addressed in this article?

The Belgic Confession of Faith, Article XXXVII

The Last Judgment

Finally, we believe, according to the Word of God, when the time appointed by the Lord (which is unknown to all creatures) is come and the number of the elect complete, that our Lord Jesus Christ will come from heaven, corporally and visibly, as He ascended, with great glory and majesty to declare Himself Judge of the living and the dead, burning this old world with fire and flame to cleanse it.[62]

To cleanse it is an appropriate end to this coming "New Earth" which is more properly read as a renewal of the earth and theologically can be seen as the lifting of the curse through the purification of fire.

Then all men will personally appear before this great Judge, both men and women and children that have been from the beginning of the world to the end thereof, being summoned by the voice of the archangel, and by the sound of the trump of God. For all the dead shall be raised out of the earth, and their souls joined and united with their proper bodies in which they formerly lived. As for those who shall then be living, they shall not die as the others, but be changed in the twinkling of an eye, and from corruptible become incorruptible. Then the books [(that is to say, the consciences)] shall be opened, and the dead judged according to what they shall have done in this world, whether it be good or evil. Nay, all men shall give account of every idle word they have spoken, which the world only counts amusement and jest; and then the secrets and hypocrisy of men shall be disclosed and laid open before all.

The choice of conscience for books here is a good one. Every

[62] HC Q57 - H XXVI all - WCF XXXII 1;2;3 - WSC Q37 - WLC Q84 thru Q87

person with total clarity will see everything they have done which condemns them before a holy God. However I do not agree this applies to the saints who are standing as over comers of the world and the flesh in faith. The conscience of the evil will condemn them so completely not one will utter a word of defense in the condemnation to hell forever. The believer however is here for reward alone. The sins have been washed in the blood of Christ, they have been covered and nothing other than God could uncover them and God will not. The bible says the sins have been removed as far as the east is from the west and that where there is no imputation of sin, there is no sin. Love covers a multitude of sins would be of no value were in that final day all was to be uncovered.

> And therefore the consideration of this judgment is justly terrible and dreadful to the wicked and ungodly, but most desirable and comfortable to the righteous and elect; because then their full deliverance shall be perfected, and there they shall receive the fruits of their labor and trouble, which they have borne. Their innocence shall be known to all, and they shall see the terrible vengeance which God shall execute on the wicked, who most cruelly persecuted, oppressed, and tormented them in this world, and who shall be convicted by the testimony of their own consciences, and shall become immortal, but only to be tormented in the eternal fire which is prepared for the devil and his angels.

Here we see part of what I said in the last paragraph. That is, who among us is going to be comfortable knowing that our every idle word is to be laid bare before a holy God in public or private? The righteousness of Christ is imputed and our own sins are not imputed. That ends that debate!

> But on the contrary, the faithful and elect shall be crowned with glory and honor; and the Son of God will confess their names before God His Father and His elect angels; all tears shall be wiped from their eyes; and their cause which is now condemned by many judges and magistrates as heretical and impious will then be known to be

the cause of the Son of God. And for a gracious reward, the Lord will cause them to possess such a glory as never entered into the heart of man to conceive.

Amen! Many of these things are happening even as this is being committed to this paper. That is Christ has already prayed for us (John 17) and is sitting at the right hand of the Father as our Mediator even Now. The Holy Spirit has brought the shadow of this future joy and even now is praying those prayers we don't know we need or how to pray. All will be made perfect or complete in that day and we shall rein with Christ forever.

> Therefore we expect that great day with a most ardent desire, to the end that we may fully enjoy the promises of God in Christ Jesus our Lord. AMEN. Amen, come, Lord Jesus.   Rev. 22:20.

If the error of the conscience of the believer bearing the full guilt of every idle word were in sight here who among men would so eagerly wait for this great day? God is gracious and our sins have been washed away completely in the acceptance by God of the completed work of Jesus Christ. In Christ we are holy and righteous and may joyfully pray this prayer of triumph in all times and circumstances.

Of not note here but interesting nonetheless is that none of the so-called "Millennium" positions can lay its foundation to this statement. The Reformed forefathers were for the most part silent here, and while they affirmed the last day and judgment of the world, they did not add to it all the baggage the church since that day.

Questions

1. Why does the [C]confession say Christ will burn this old world at His coming?

2. What will be perfected for believers at the coming of Christ?

3. Why do believers ardently await the coming of the Lord without fear?

About the Author

Dr. Baynard was born in Kings Mountain, North Carolina in the waning days of WWII as the fourth son of Doyle C. Baynard, Sr. and Dorothy Mae Woody Baynard. The family moved to Wadesboro, NC when he was four, which proved to be the final move of a hitherto itinerant life. His father's employment in the cotton industry meant often moving in an attempt to better provide for the growing family.

Anson County in the 50s was all cotton farmers and cotton mills. A huge percentage of the population lived at or below the poverty level. At seventeen Chuck joined the U.S. Army to escape what appeared to be a dead end life in a cotton mill. He spent the next twelve years in assignments on all four corners of the globe to include two years as a Green Beret in the Republic of South Viet Nam.

In 1972 he left the service with an AA degree in electronics in hand and began his own business in Clover, SC. In 1982 he was called of God to enter the ministry. He began as a Commissioned Lay Pastor, a position that appears to be unique with the PCUSA. This position differed from ordained minister in that educational requirements were waived and the person so commissioned could serve as pastor of a church, to include the serving of the sacraments. Chuck spent four years in this position providing pulpit supply to many small churches in York County, SC.

During this time he pursued the education required by the Presbyterian denominations for ordination. Eventually earning his bachelor's degree] in]theology and masters in ministry. He completed his doctor of theology with Whitefield Graduate School of Theology in the spring of 2002.

Chuck was ordained in the EPC in the fall of 1993. He is the founding evangelist (1991) and continues as the solo pastor of Clover Evangelical Presbyterian Church in Clover, SC. He is married to Mollie Adams Baynard and has one daughter Elizabeth, who teaches chemistry in Clover High School.

Chuck considers himself gifted of the Lord to reduce complex theological constructions to their simplest form so all can understand the precepts and know what they believe and why.

Other Titles Currently Available by Dr. Baynard

The ABCs of Reformed Theology
When the Mountain Thundered
Peppermint Patty Meets the C-Monster
Westminster Revisited Confession of Faith
Westminster Revisited Larger Catechism Vol I
Presbyterian Perspectives

www.lulu.com/observer

www.ingramcontent.com/pod-product-compliance
Lightning Source LLC
Chambersburg PA
CBHW032104080426
42733CB00006B/408